+F216 .C294 1990

CARIBBEAN VISIONS

CARIBBEAN VISIONS

*Ten Presidential Addresses of
Ten Presidents of the
Caribbean Studies Association*

Edited by:

S. B. JONES-HENDRICKSON

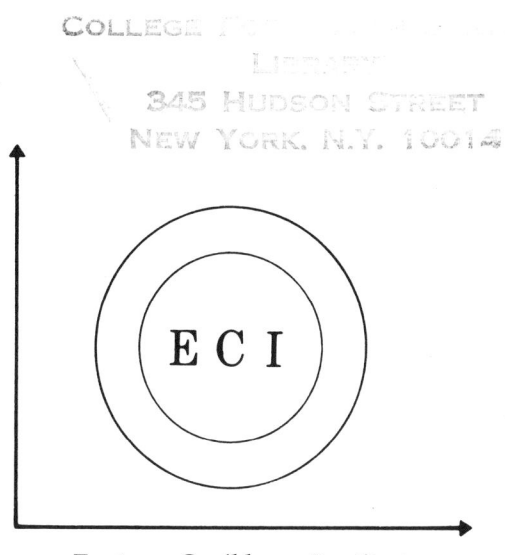

Eastern Caribbean Institute

CARIBBEAN VISIONS

Copyright 1990 by The Eastern Caribbean Institute

All rights reserved. No part of this book may be reproduced in any form by any electronic or mechanical means (including photocopying, recording, or information storage and retrieval) without permission in writing from the publisher.

Library of Congress Cataloging-in-Publication Data
Library of Congress Catalog Card Number 90-71043

Caribbean Visions

1. Essays. Presidential Addresses
I. Jones-Hendrickson, S. B.

ISBN 0-932831-06-0

EASTERN CARIBBEAN INSTITUTE
BOX 1338
FREDERIKSTED, V.I. 00841

CONTENTS

Acknowledgements   vii
Introduction—S. B. Jones-Hendrickson   ix
Contributors   xv

SECTION I

1. Equality and Social Justice: Foundations of Nationalism in the Caribbean—*Wendell Bell*   3

2. The United States and the Caribbean: The Dominant Power and the New States—*Vaughan Lewis*   47

3. Absorbing the Caribbean Labor Surplus: The Need for an Indigenous Engine of Growth—*Ransford Palmer*   71

4. The Structure of Modern-Conservative Societies—*Anthony Maingot*   89

SECTION II

5. Strategies for Progress in the Post-Independence Caribbean: A Bradshawian Synthesis—S. B. Jones-Hendrickson   121

6. Human Resources in the Caribbean—*Fuat Andic*   153

7. Economic Aspects of the Relationship Between State and People in the Caribbean—*Compton Bourne*   163

SECTION III

8. The Challenge of Leadership in the Caribbean — *Alma H. Young* — 181

9. The Caribbean, Zone Of Peace: Possible Utopia? — *Andres Serbin* — 193

10. Visions of Development Beckoning: The Caribbean Studies Association — *J. Edward Greene* — 221

11. Conclusion: *S. B. Jones-Hendrickson* — 245

ACKNOWLEDGMENTS

I want to take this opportunity to express my gratitude to nine Presidents of the Caribbean Studies Association (CSA) for permitting me to edit this volume of addresses, CARIBBEAN VISIONS, as a symbolic expression of the visions of some of the persons who led the Caribbean Studies Association for over ten years.

In this regard, I also wish to record my thanks to *Caribbean Studies* in which Wendell Bell's address first appeared. In the same vein, my thanks to Barry Levine, CSA long-standing member and Editor of *Caribbean Review*, for Vaughan Lewis' and Ransford Palmer's addresses. Thanks, also, to Ransford Palmer for permission to use his article from his book, *Problems of Development in Beautiful Countries*, North-South, 1984. To Westview Press, thanks; Anthony Maingot address appeared in Jack Knippers Black (Editor), *Latin America, Its Problems and Its Promise: A Multidisciplinary Introduction*, West View Press, 1984. Fuat Andic's and Andres Serbin's addresses appeared in the Caribbean Studies Association Newsletter. My thanks to CSA and the Newsletter Editors Alma H. Young and Jacqueline Braveboy-Wagner. My address on Robert L. Bradshaw appeared in a serialized form in the *Labour Spokesman*, of St. Kitts, in the month of May, 1984. My thanks to the *Labour Spokesman*.

My thanks to Sandra Thomas who organized the documents before transferring to the St. Thomas campus of the University of the Virgin Islands and thereby deprived me of her efficient organizational services. My best to her as a potential CSA member.

There is an all encompassing thank you to the many CSA friends, colleagues and buddies who expressed great enthusiasm when I first broached them with this idea of editing the addresses of the CSA Presidents. In their enthusiasm they gave me the added fillip to move on with the book.

Finally, in the line of thank you, a big thank you to my spouse, Cora L. E. Christian, CSA Health Panel coordinator, since 1976 in Guadeloupe, and thanks to our children, Nesha and Marcus, who constantly wonder why I have to stay up till four in the mornings, night after night. The patience and understanding of my family are appreciated.

Many publishers expressed interest in the book (we thank them); but, the publishers' schedules took them from here to eternity. In my usual way, I did my Keynesian approach to the book. Whatever contribution CARIBBEAN VISIONS may make to Caribbean scholarship, Caribbean scholars, Caribbeanists and others who are interested in the developments in the Caribbean, is a contribution that I will willing share with my CSA family and friends. CARIBBEAN VISIONS is from one CSA family to all other members of the wider CSA family and friends.

INTRODUCTION

In 1973 I left the University of Exeter, England, and took up a position as Assistant Lecturer in Economics at the University of the West Indies, Mona, Jamaica. The next year, 1974, we started an involvement in Caribbean meetings. In that same year I received an invitation from one Roland I. Perusse to join an association of Caribbeanists. I remembered wondering who Roland I. Perusse was and how he got my name. I responded positively to the invitation and eventually attended the First Organizational Meeting and Conference of the Caribbean Studies Association at the Hotel Boriquen, San Juan, Puerto Rico, from Wednesday, January 8 to Saturday, January 11, 1975.

The theme of the Conference was *Patterns of Change in the Contemporary Caribbean*. At that Meeting and Conference, there were 21 panels, five plenary sessions, and a luncheon meeting, in addition to the President's reception, inaugural meeting of the CSA Council and the Business Meeting.

The elected officers of the CSA Council were Roland I. Perusse, President, Inter-American University of Puerto Rico; Basil A. Ince, Vice President, Institute of International Relations, University of the West Indies, St. Augustine; Carlos Albizu-Miranda, Caribbean Center for Advanced Study, San Juan, Puerto Rico; Angel Calderon Cruz, University of Puerto Rico; John Figueroa, Caribbean Center for Advanced Study; Abraham Lowenthal, Council on Foreign Relations, New York City; David Lowenthal, University College, London; Carmelo Mesa-Lago, University of Pittsburgh and Annemarie de Waal Malefijt, Hunter College, New York. There was no elected Secretary-Treasurer.

On the second day of the meeting, Roland Perusse approached me and asked me if I would like to be an officer of the CSA. I said I would like to contribute as an officer. He said that the position of Secretary-Treasurer was open and that he was going to propose my name to the Council to be the CSA Secretary-Treasurer. The inaugural meeting of the Council of the Caribbean Studies Association was held in Suite 2505–06, Hotel Borinquen, and I was nominated to be the first Secretary-Treasurer of the CSA.

On March 17, 1975, the Third Council Meeting of the CSA was held at the Eastern Airlines Conference Room, San Juan International Airport. I attended my first official meeting and on June 13, 1975 I presented my first set of minutes and Secretary-Treasurer's report. Also present at the meeting were Perusse, Basil Ince, Carlos Albizu-Miranda, John Figueroa, Angel Calderon Cruz. We had Income of $4,231.63 and expenses of $4,079.63 for a balance of $152. CSA has come a long way from those days.

It is instructive to note some of the persons who were listed and who attended the first meeting of CSA in January, 1975. Panel one, "Theory for Caribbean Economy," was chaired by Steve DeCastro, then my colleague at UWI, Jamaica. Among his panelists was Courtney Blackman, then Governor of the Central Bank of Barbados. In panel two, "Metropolitan Ties and Influences," Ramesh Ramsarran, ISER, Mona, another colleague, was a panelist. Clive Thomas, University of Guyana, was a discussant. Ransford W. Palmer, Howard University, chaired a panel on "Economic Policies—External." Rawle Farley, then of SUNY at Brockport, Aubrey Armstrong at Fisk University, and Vincent McDonald, Howard University were panelists; Harley Hinricks, Howard University was a discussant.

Alan Eyre, UWI, Mona, chaired a panel on "Population Dynamics." Among the panelists were Henry E. Lamur, University of Amsterdam, William Stinner, Pennsylvania and Klaus de Albuquerque, Wofford College. Frank Paul Le Veness, St. John's University, chaired a panel on "Politics in the

Commonwealth Caribbean." Panelists were W. Anderson and Rudolph Grant, York University, Canada; Marvin Will, University of Tulsa and Maurice Waters, Wayne State University.

"Foreign Policies of the Caribbean" was chaired by Arpad von Lazar of the Fletcher School of Diplomacy. Basil Ince, UWI, St. Augustine, Angel Calderon Cruz, University of Puerto Rico, and Leslie Manigat, UWI, St. Augustine, were among the panelists. Roberta Johnson, University of Missouri was among the discussants.

Fuat Andic, University of Puerto Rico, chaired a panel on "Economic Policies – Internal." Among the panelists were Michael S. Joshua, SUNY at Buffalo; S. B. Jones-Hendrickson, UWI, Mona; Arthur Mann, University of Puerto Rico, Mayaguez; John Belcher, University of Georgia. Discussants included Gary Olson, Moravian College; Sydney E. Chernick, Washington, D. C.; Aaron Segal, Cornell University; Richard Jolly, University of Sussex; Owen Jefferson, Caribbean Development Bank (on secondment from UWI, Mona) and Francis O. Riviere, East Caribbean Common Market, Antigua.

A panel on "Dependency and Independence in the Caribbean" was chaired by J. E. Greene, UWI, Mona. Among the panelists were Carl Parris, UWI, St. Augustine, Jean Crusol, CERAG, Martinique and Rosina Wiltshire, UWI, Mona. Rudolph Grant, York University, Canada, was the discussant.

Randolph Williams, UWI, Mona chaired a panel on "Econometric Modelling." Steve DeCastro presented results on his famous "Turnpike model" for Jamaica. I was a discussant for Randy William's paper on "Tax Incentives and Investment in Developing Countries: The Case of the Cement Industry in Jamaica."

Locksley Edmondson, UWI, Mona, chaired a panel on "Relations with the Third World." Vaughan Lewis, ISER, UWI, Jamaica, the late Adlith Brown, and Locksley were panelists; Earle Scarlett, Loyola Marymount University was the discussant.

Others who I met at that First CSA Conference and Meeting were DeLisle Worrell, Central Bank of Barbados; Roy Simon Bryce-Laporte, who was at the Smithsonian Institution; the late Richard Frucht, University of Alberta, Canada and Jerome Handler, Southern Illinois University. Olive Senior, then Publications Editor of *Social and Economic Studies*, also attended the meeting.

At that same meeting I had the opportunity to meet Sybil and Gordon Lewis, names I had known but faces I did not know. I also met Archie Singham. The circumstances under which I met Sybil, Gordon and Archie were rather peculiar. I was invited to attend a "Counter CSA Conference" at the home of Sybil and Gordon Lewis. I remember, distinctly, the discussions which were held in Gordon's study. (There were mounds of newspapers). The main substance of the discussions was that CSA could not really be construed as a Caribbean organization. The contention was that we, Caribbean people, should disassociate ourselves from CSA. There was no general consensus on the charge of the cloud over CSA. I left the meeting with no clear-cut ideas. I made a decision, however, that I will continue to be part of CSA and make sure that CSA continues to be a Caribbean Association, as the name states.

Out of that inaugural 1975 CSA meeting, many of the CSA founding members went on to play active roles in the development and growth of CSA. Basil Ince became President; Angel Calderon Cruz was a many facetted person in CSA (Acting President, President, Secretary Treasurer and Program Chairman); Vaughan Lewis, Ransford Palmer, Fuat Andic, Eddie and I were Presidents. Carl Parris was a two-time Program Chairman; Klaus de Albuquerque was a Program Chairman. Frank Paul Le Veness and Marvin Will were Newsletter editors.

In the early years, the concept of a Presidential Address

was not institutionalized. Wendell Bell, CSA President 1979-1980, presented the first Presidential Address, in Curacao, Netherlands Antilles, May 1980. From that time, the CSA Presidential Address has become a staple of the Annual CSA Conference.

CARIBBEAN VISIONS is a collection of ten presidential addresses of ten Presidents of the Caribbean Studies Association. CSA is now the premier organization that studies that Caribbean. The ten addresses, this introduction and a conclusion comprise the main parts of the book. We have also included a short biography of each President. The book provides an assessment of the legacy of the Caribbean Studies Association to the people of the Caribbean in the Caribbean and the diaspora. CARIBBEAN VISIONS is a book of visions of and for the Caribbean by some of the many leaders who have decided to master an understanding of the social and political dynamics of the Caribbean.

It is my view that CARIBBEAN VISIONS has something to offer to a variety of persons, in that the volume records important essays from an international array of scholars. The addresses are on a broad variety of topics. The topics offer visions of and for the Caribbean. Seen in their proper perspective, these visions will transcend time and space.

Given the nature of the topics covered in the ten addresses, CARIBBEAN VISIONS is truly global in its scope and scale. Consequently, the volume should find usage among persons in Economics, Sociology, Politics, Social Problems, Caribbean issues in a broad sense, and Third World issues in a large sense.

CARIBBEAN VISIONS is divided in three sections. In section one, there are four addresses. The addresses are:

1. "Equality and Social Justice: Foundations of Nationalism in the Caribbean." – Wendell Bell

2. "The United States and the Caribbean: The Dominant Power and the New States." – Vaughan Lewis
3. "Absorbing the Caribbean Labor Surplus: The Need for an Indigenous Engine of Growth." – Ransford Palmer
4. "The Structure of Modern-Conservative Societies." – Anthony Maingot

The second section is comprised of three addresses. These are:

5. "Strategies for Progress in the Post-Independence Caribbean: A Bradshawian Synthesis." – S. B. Jones-Hendrickson
6. "Human Resources in the Caribbean" – Fuat Andic
7. "Economic Aspects of the Relationship Between State and People in the Caribbean" – Compton Bourne

The third section is comprised of three papers:

8. "The Challenge of Leadership in the Caribbean" – Alma H. Young
9. "The Caribbean, Zone of Peace: Possible Utopia?" – Andres Serbin
10. "Visions of Development Beckoning: The Caribbean Studies Association" – J. Edward Greene

In the final analysis, CARIBBEAN VISIONS is offered in the manner and style in which the addresses were first presented to the CSA audiences. Even in those cases where the addresses were published before, the substance of the addresses is still true to form. It is our view that CARIBBEAN VISIONS will fill a good spot in the historical legacy of charting those visions of and for the people in the Caribbean, Caribbeanists and others who are interested in developments in the Caribbean.

CONTRIBUTORS

Wendell Bell	Professor of Sociology, Yale University; CSA President, 1979-80
Vaughan Lewis	Director-General, Organization of Eastern Caribbean States and former Director of the Institute of Social and Economic Research, UWI, Jamaica; CSA President, 1980-81
Ransford Palmer	Professor of Economics, Howard University; CSA President, 1981-82
Anthony Maingot	Professor of Sociology, Florida International University; CSA President, 1982-83
SBJH*	Professor of Economics, University of the Virgin Islands, St. Croix; CSA President, 1983-84
Fuat Andic	Professor of Economics, (formerly), University of Puerto Rico, Rio Piedras; CSA President, 1984-85
Compton Bourne	Professor of Economics, University of the West Indies, St. Augustine, Trinidad; CSA President, 1985-86
Alma H. Young	Professor of Urban Studies and Public Affairs, University of New Orleans; CSA President, 1986-87

Andres Serbin   Professor of Sociology and International
                             Relations and Director, Venezuelan
                             Institute of Social and Political Studies;
                             CSA President, 1987–88.

J. Edward Greene   Pro-Vice Chancellor, and Director,
                             Institute of Social and Economic Research,
                             UWI, Mona Jamaica; CSA President,
                             1988–89

*S. B. Jones-Hendrickson, Editor

SECTION I

Equity and Social Justice: Foundations of Nationalism in the Caribbean

WENDELL BELL

My purpose in this article is to examine the foundations of nationalism in the Caribbean, especially in the new states that have been created since the end of the Second World War. I try to place the new states of the Caribbean in time and space, showing where they fit into the broad trends of nationalism since the middle of the eighteenth century and into the global diffusion of modern nationalism from Europe and North America, to Latin America, to Africa and Asia, and to the Caribbean and the Pacific.

My first thesis is that, for the new nationalist leaders, political independence was the means to achieve the goal of the reduction of civil, political, economic, social, and cultural inequalities. That is, grasping control of the legitimate power of the state was viewed as instrumental to transforming society so as to achieve social justice. Given the obvious inequalities of colonialism and the then-current definitions of the fairness of certain equalities both within the metropole and the colonies, the weight of moral judgment tended to support the historical actions of 20th century nationalist leaders in their struggles for political independence.

My second thesis is that social justice does not inherently mean equality. Depending on the circumstances, many inequalities may be judged as fair by members of society. I give considerable attention to this point in an effort to clarify the distinctions between the two concepts of equality and equity, because they are so often confused.

The distinctions are key to my main argument, the third thesis, that in the final analysis it is social justice or equity — not equality — that political regimes ought to be seeking if they wish to minimize political alienation among their citizens and to create and maintain their legitimacy. In other words, governmental policies producing or failing to change both unfair equalities and unfair inequalities may bring down a regime.

In the Caribbean today, as elsewhere, threats to the stability of the political and social orders can be found in the ineffectiveness and inefficiency of political regimes. Threats also come from inequities, importantly both from inequalities that are judged by some members of society to be unfair and from efforts to create equalities that are judged by other members of society as unfair. Of course, this fact helps to explain why ideological — as distinct from pragmatic — politics often become confrontations between different groups of true believers, each righteously committed to what they believe to be moral, though opposing, principles.

THE RISE OF THE NEW STATES

The creation of new states must be included among the half dozen or so momentous world-changing events that occurred during the three and a half decades of the mid-twentieth century. At the beginning of World War II there were 70 nation-states. Today, excluding some territories that may be too small to be considered a state, there are about 160, approximately 90 of which have attained the political status of independent sovereign state during the last 35 years. The rapidity of the change is breathtaking. There has been an average of two and one-half new states formed during each year of the last 35.

Today, the state-founding process has nearly run its course. Only a few colonial territories remain from which additional new states can be made, and a few more may be carved from existing states if separatist movements are successful, e.g., Basque Spain or French Canada. For the first time in history, practically all peoples everywhere on earth live under the rule of "their own" nation-state. The zenith of the age of nationalism has been reached, where some state demands and receives the highest loyalty of its people and where the state claims legitimate domination over all other institutions of its society.

Most of the new states were formed out of the former European colonies in Asia and Africa, fewer from the Pacific. But the Caribbean also participated in the process with the creation of ten new states. In August 1962, Jamaica became the first new state in the Western Hemisphere since Panama in 1903. Trinidad and Tobago followed closely, also in August of 1962. Since then, Guyana and Barbados in 1966, the Bahamas in 1973, Grenada in 1974, Suriname in 1975, Dominica in 1978, and St. Lucia and St. Vincent and the Grenadines in 1979 joined the ranks of the new national political entities. A few others wait hesitantly in the wings, such as the six islands of the Netherlands Antilles and a few remaining British territories. Others, at least for the time being, remain self-governing in association with another state, e.g., Puerto Rico with the United States; and still others moved toward fuller political integration with the metropole rather than seeking independence, as in the case of Guadeloupe and Martinique with France.

The Caribbean colonies generally experienced heavier burdens of political, economic, social and cultural domination than the Asian and African colonies. For example, they remained under imperialism far longer, indigenous people and cultures were penetrated more fully and often destroyed, and three hundred years of slavery and then indentured labor, based on race and ethnicity, made deeper the wounds of exploitation, deprivation and inequality. The importation of indentured labor to the Caribbean continued until about the first quarter of the twentieth century.

NATIONALISM AND THE DEMOCRATIC REVOLUTION

Hayes (1950), Kohn (1957, 1965) and many other writers have demonstrated the importance of the latter half of the eighteenth century as the period and Europe as the place of the rise of modern nationalism. That period coincides, of course, with the rise and initial spread of the democratic revolution throughout Europe and its North American colonies, as is shown by Palmer (1959, 1965). Palmer documents the diffusion through a number of countries of different parts of a single movement with unifying characteristics. It included the increase in the scale of society by the inclusion of an even larger percentage of adults within the borders of the emergent states, with each person sharing a basic equality of national citizenship, an equal expectation of universal loyalty and responsibility to the state, and a commitment to the principle of liberty. Political democracy and modern nationalism were two linked processes in the integration of the masses of people into a common political form.

The first part of the nineteenth century witnessed the diffusion of the democratic revolution into Latin American while the second half of the twentieth saw its spectacular spread into the former colonies of Asia, Africa, the Pacific, and most of the remaining colonies of the Caribbean. Haiti had become independent in 1804 during the first wave, the Dominican Republic in 1844 during the second, and Cuba in 1901, a delayed second wave state, and the new states of the Caribbean listed above during the third wave.

This is not to say that people suffering the oppression of colonial inequalities could not—or did not—invent the ideology of the justice of equality and the liberating acts of their own deliverance. They surely did, hundreds of times. But the links between such ideas across space and time often constituted networks of communication and influence that preserved and activated the conceptions of social justice embodied in the democratic ideal and gave them life through historical action.

During the two hundred years from the latter part of the 18th to the latter part of the 20th century, the implications of Enlightenment and democratic thought were defined, redefined, and expanded. In pre-revolutionary North America—in what was to become, as Lipset (1963) has called it, the first new nation—most liberal thinkers regarded themselves as republicans, advocated a system of government in which officials derived their authority from an electorate (then of quite limited and varying sizes), and assumed that legitimacy of government rested on the people's will (Alger, 1972: 58). The term "democracy" itself, however, and the idea of people's direct political participation still referred to mob rule or anarchy and were more negatively than positively valued, even though one can recognize the democratic inclinations of the struggle against both tyranny and the ideology of the divine right of kings.

Questions of economic and social equality were simply not much on the scene in pre-revolutionary America, where it was taken for granted that "People of about the same social or economic position ought to pretty much mingle with their own kind." This was a question that I asked Jamaican leaders in 1958 and that many of them, especially pronationalist leaders, rejected. But according to Alger even Sam Adams, a revolutionary American who was accused of preferring the company of ropewalkers to men of his own station, would not have agreed with the statement in 18th century America. Issues at the time dealt primarily with civil and political equality; for example, the right to worship in a church of one's own choosing without negative sanction. Notions of representation, consent of the governed, constitutionalism, and individual rights were beginning a long process of specification and elaboration. It would take later generations to add universal adult suffrage and the ideas of the justice of economic and social equality.

Yet Alger's study of American pre-revolutionary leaders supports the contention that national movements originating in colonial settings were inspired by liberal ideals which had their origin in the European Enlightenment. She finds (p. 265), for example, that American leaders who believed that it was more important to preserve liberty rather than authority in a time of challenge to the established order, who believed that it was the rules and not the ruled who were the most likely source of despotism, and who thought the people and not the leaders displayed the best judgment in matters of government, were more likely to favor American independence from Britain than were American leaders who believed the opposite, by 83 to 14 percent.

THE CAUSES OF NATIONALISM IN THE 20TH CENTURY

Alger's findings are consistent with the propositions formulated by myself and my associates in our studies of the transition to political independence of the new states of the English-speaking Caribbean.[1] Under what conditions, we asked, would a people under foreign rule organize a nationalist movement? We defined a nationalist movement as a collection of people who exhibited organized politico-social beliefs, attitudes, emotions, and actions aimed at the creation of a nation-state, politically independent and autonomous, self-governing, and geographically distinct.

Our studies showed that nationalist movements with significant following would form:

(1) If clear-cut inequalities (civil, political, economic, social or cultural) exist between the local or "indigenous" inhabitants, i.e., the people typical of a territory on the one hand, and the representatives or agents of a foreign power on the other hand, where such inequalities are institutionalized, legitimated, and enforced by imperial political rule and where what is "indigenous" as opposed to "foreign" may be defined on the basis of race, ethnicity, religion, or emergent nationality.
(2) If such inequalities are perceived by a critical number of local people; that is, if indigenous people become conscious of them.
(3) If there exists within the value system of the local people a judgment of such inequalities as unjust; that is, if there exist values favorable to liberty, equality, and fraternity.
(4) If there is an elite among the local people that is both committed to such values and capable of mobilizing the material and organizational resources necessary to sustain a social movement.
(5) If changes toward a more just society, defined as more egalitarian, are believed by a sufficient number of local people to be impossible, too difficult, or too slow in coming under the existing politically dependent status.
(6) If political independence is perceived as feasible by at least a core of local leaders, in the sense both of successfully attaining political separation from the imperial power and of successfully becoming a viable political, economic, and social unit after independence.

(7) If there exists at least a core of local culture identifiably separate from the culture of the imperial power.

Note that these propositions are "if" statements, not "if and only if" statements. That is, they are sufficient conditions only, not necessary conditions. When they occur, we predict a nationalist movement will occur, i.e., they are sufficient to produce it. For nearly all of the new states, these conditions were met and nationalist movements were formed that were successful in achieving political independence. But other conditions may also produce a nationalist movement, as in the case of the 1965 unilateral declaration of independence on the part of the white settlers of Rhodesia, an exclusive, undemocratic movement of a minority section of the population that faced potential internal democratic reforms forced on it from Britain. It is only now, after the reaction has been negated, that the inclusive, universal democratic forces—in what is now Zimbabwe—have a chance to control the direction of history.

The above propositions concern the outcome of the first of a series of "decisions of nationhood" that we formulated as a framework for understanding the images of the future and the historical actions of colonial and new nationalist leaders, among others, in the former British Caribbean and elsewhere. Other decisions of nationhood concern the desired amount of national sovereignty, location of the geographic boundaries of the emergent state, the consilience of the state in the political sense with the nation in the cultural sense, the form of government—Western democracy or not, the role of the state in the economy and the society, the national character of the people, the nature of the social structure— especially egalitarian or not, the content of the new state national culture, and finally, the external affairs and global alignments of the new state.[2]

THE RISING DOMINANCE OF THE EGALITARIAN REVOLUTION

An important shift occurred from the 18th to the 20th century transforming what had been primarily a democratic revolution into an egalitarian revolution. From stressing liberty, the demands changed, increasingly emphasizing equality. This is not so much revealed by the fate of political democracy in the new states, where I note that about four-fifth entered nationhood with Western-style democratic regimes while fewer than half remain democracies in this sense today, as it is by the change in the conception of what inequalities were considered unfair and what equalities came to be judged as normally expected of a just society.[3] Certainly today advanced thinkers of the new states include in their images of the just society:

(1) equality of opportunity for nearly all economic, social and cultural goods;
(2) minimum levels of economic survival and even comfort below which no one in the society ought to be permitted to fall; and
(3) a full set of economic, social, and cultural rights, ranging from the right to work, to the right to family life and free choice of a marriage partner, to the right to express freely one's religion and cultural preferences. This is not to say that the debate over what equalities or inequalities are fair is over. By no means is that so. It remains an important problem. But what is taken for granted as minimally agreed upon egalitarian expectations today which have been considered at least mildly insane in the latter half of the 18th century.

Nothing struck us more forcibly in our pre-independence research in the English-speaking Caribbean than the pronationalist leaders' concern over the many hurtful inequalities of race and class under colonialism and their images of a more just, egalitarian future. They wanted to get control of the state, ending British political domination, so that they could use the state as an instrument to lessen inequality. The anti-nationalists, to the contrary, nearly all judged many of the same inequalities to be fair.

Reading V.S. Naipaul and other cynics of modern change in the Caribbean, one might suspect that such pro-nationalist statements were the empty rhetoric of poseurs and look for the truth in the shadows of secret behavior and in the dark corners of hidden, and probably twisted, psyches.

Our re-study of economic and social indicators, social legislation, and elite attitudes in Jamaica twelve years after independence, however, does not sustain such a jaundiced view (Bell, 1977; Bell and Stevenson, 1979; Robinson and Bell, 1978a). True, income inequality has stubbornly remained, unemployment and underemployment rates have stayed high, and poor relief has become barely more adequate than before independence. Yet changes have occurred. Improvements were intended by legislation dealing with minimum wages, workmen's compensation, pensions, medical services, literacy, egalitarian tax reform, land-lease, and free primary education. More equality was achieved in primary education and school enrollments were up. Of course, where expenditures were necessary, Jamaica's precarious— and now desperate—financial situation prevented the achievement of many egalitarian reforms without severe reductions in the wealth of others. Yet the sincerity of egalitarian visions of social justice can be seen in those acts of Jamaican leaders that were within their power to perform. An important example is the change of laws reducing inequalities between members of legal and "extra-legal" families and between legitimate and "illegitimate" children. In a country where 70 percent of all children are born out of a legal marriage, the elimination of the legal disabilities of being a "bastard" and the banishment of the term itself from legal documents have been important acts creating more equality. Another example is the extraordinary increase in cultural appreciation of things Jamaican and Caribbean and of the African origins of the majority of the people. The will for egalitarian reforms was—and is—there, even though the economic resources, organizational skills, or good luck for creating more economic equality at acceptable levels of living have not always been forthcoming.

One important methodological consideration should be kept in mind when evaluating the performance of new nationalist elites in bringing about egalitarian reforms. Although less salient than the goal of equality in the rhetoric of nationalist leaders before independence, another obvious goal of political independence was increasing the size of the economic pie, i.e., raising the average level of living of people within the emergent state. Of course, there is no necessary relationship between the average level of a variable and the degree of inequality of a variable, using, for example, the variance as a measure of inequality. Yet there are times in actual situations when they are at odds. For example, in a new state in which there are few university graduates, a reasonable policy aimed at increasing wealth and raising levels of living through increased capacity for development might include expanding opportunities for higher education, building a university, or providing scholarships for some students to obtain higher education abroad. Other things being equal, the results of such policies—that is, adding new high levels of education for some people—would increase the average level of education in the country and at the same time increase educational inequality.

A number of important variables involved in development behave in exactly this way. Increasing inequality is often a byproduct of increasing levels of skill—and of comfort and privilege as well-for some groups and not for others, at least in the early stages of development where resources are limited as, of course, they nearly always are. This is not a matter of debate; it is a statistical fact.[4] Yet, such a process of uneven advantage may be necessary for the sake of development and eventual achievement of more equality at higher levels of living for all. Everyone and everything can seldom be changed overnight. In the example given, if the new and expanded group of university graduates, after their own educations were completed, were deployed as teachers to help raise the minimum levels of education for the least educated sections of society, then, eventually, not only would average educational levels be raised, but also inequality of education would be reduced.

THE WORLD-WIDE TREND TOWARD EQUALITY

The new states came center stage over the last generation. Their leaders entered the international community of states, proclaimed their egalitarian images of a just future, established the nonaligned group of nations, created the Third— and, some say, the Fourth—Worlds, and pursued their hopes for social justice within the international economic order as well as on the domestic scene. Our sight, however, should not be blinded by these events to the point where we fail to see the connections between the images of the future of new nationalist leaders and the guiding images and actions of people who sought social changes in the old states during the same period of time. There has been a worldwide call for more equality. The Welsh and Scottish nationalists in Great Britain; Basques and Catalans in Spain; the

Flemish in Belgium; Bretons in France; Ukrainians, Crimean Tatars and Jews in the Soviet Union; Catholics in Northern Ireland; Native Americans and French-Canadians in Canada; Native-Americans, Hispanics, and Blacks in the United States . . ., the list goes on and on.

We forget, perhaps, both the limitations on civil and other human rights that existed within the older states at the end of World War II and the rather remarkable and rapid changes that have occurred since. Take the United States as one example. During the early 1950s, while Jamaica and Trinidad were preparing the ground for civil and democratic change, the United States was wracked by McCarthyism. Those were the days when in Southern California one could see bumper stickers reading "Kill a Commie for Christ." They were days of racial discrimination, of black fear, and in the American South of lynchings for which no "perpetrators" would be found or punished.

But change had already begun. On May 17, 1954 the U.S. Supreme Court in the Brown vs. Board of Education of Topeka, Kansas decision held that enforced racial segregation of public education was a denial of the equal protection of the laws guaranteed under the 14th Amendment. One doesn't know whether to celebrate the event or to feel shame that it came so late in the life of what some people still believe to be one of the greatest democracies of the world. Then, in 1957, the country was electrified by a violent confrontation at Central High School in Little Rock, Arkansas. Governor Orval Faubus defied the federal government's order to integrate the school. We watched President Eisenhower on national television where he declared,

> The very basis of our individual rights and freedoms rests upon the certainty that the President and the executive branch of government will support and insure the carrying out of the decisions of the federal courts, even, when neces-

sary, with all the means at the President's command. Unless the President did so, anarchy would result (Manchester, 1975: 985).

Secretary of Defense Wilson had earlier placed the Arkansas National Guard in federal service, out of control of Governor Faubus, and, as Ike spoke on television, the first trucks carrying paratroopers of a crack combat outfit, the 327th Battle Group of the 101st Airborne Division, were rolling up in front of Central High. The nine black children over whom the confrontation occurred entered Central High and they stayed. To see these things was to witness the wall of inequality being breached. Although some months later that story was history, a final battle for racial equality in the United States had begun, the antagonists engaged.

Before it ended—and, of course, it has not fully ended even today—other fighters included Autherine Lucy, James Meredith, Medgar Evers and Stokely Carmichael; Martin Luther King and his Southern Christian Leadership Conference; Malcolm X and the Black Nationalist Party; CORE and SNCC; Eldridge Cleaver and James Baldwin; H. Rap Brown and Huey P. Newton; scores of freedom riders, marchers, boycotters, and sit-ins. And, of course, a quiet, then 42-year-old lady named Rosa Parks who, being in tune with the future, simply wouldn't give up her seat to a white man on a Montgomery, Alabama bus. These, too, and the changes they brought forth are now history.

The Civil Rights Act of 1964 was a major victory and the subsequent implementation of affirmative action programs in education and occupation in the 1970s for both American minority group members and women brings us up to date with the trend toward social justice through increasing equality within the United States. And what of Little Rock? By 1974, Central High had a black principal. By 1976, a black student body president was elected by votes both of black and white students who by 1978 were not only fully integrated, but also were in the mood to celebrate their victory over inequality in a documentary motion picture.[5] Black consciousness in America had been aroused and fundamentally changed and it was linked to the decolonization of black Africa which had begun in the late 1950s.

And I hear echoes of other voices: Nanny of the Maroons, Sam Sharpe, Paul Bogle, William George Gordon, Marcus Garvey, Alexander Bustamante, Norman W. Manley, to mention the national heroes of only one new Caribbean state; heroes who, in the present of things past, to use St. Augustine's phrase, are now viewed as having led a struggle for equality.

Thus, some changes in many of the old states, such as illustrated for the United States, have paralleled and were sometimes intertwined with changes in the new states as social justice was redefined in wider and wider terms, prominently including equalities of various kinds, as it was fought for, and as it was achieved.[6] For the new states, including those of the Caribbean, the struggle for egalitarian reforms during the last generation has been fundamental to the meaning of new national sovereignty itself, since it occurred in the context of the transfer of state power from one group to another and since the state was viewed as a chief mechanism for its achievement. Moreover, for the old states, it would be accurate to say something similar: their very meaning is given in their charter myths, such as America's Declaration of Independence, and their grasp of equality came closer to their reach as a result of the egalitarian changes of the last thirty years.

Some readers may find it difficult to rationalize this view of the United States and other old, powerful states with their behavior abroad. For example, the "trashy tactics" of the United States in other countries are well known (Crile, 1974). We now know of the duplicities, briberies, abductions, and assassinations that official agents of the United States attempted or succeeded in carrying out or arranging. We know of the secret wars and the covert operations that the United States has conducted. We know of the American efforts to prevent Allende from taking power in Chile though he was democratically elected. Many people have reason to believe that the general policy of the United States in the Caribbean was—and still may be—as ex-CIA agent Philip Agee (1975: 7) has said, "to repress the left and prop up those governments which are favorable to U.S. interests . . . which means the penetration, division, weakening and defeat of those groups which indicate economic nationalism and of left-wing groups. Those are the targets in other words, because the CIA sees the local scene as divided between the friendlies and the enemies."

There are contradictions in American official behavior—egalitarian reforms through law at home and reactionary, even illegal, tactics abroad that violate minimum conceptions of human dignity. One can speculate that the egalitarian revolution may continue to spread until it governs the relations *among* nations as well as the relationships *within* nations. With respect to may example of the United States in the Caribbean, there is some evidence from my conversations with U.S. State Department officials and from others (Crile, 1974) of a change in U.S. policies under President Carter toward less of a patronizing attitude, less intervention, less concern with the nature of social change internal to the countries involved if it genuinely expresses the will of the people there, and certainly less interest in trying to manage change. Whether or not this change will become a long-term feature of U.S. policy toward the Caribbean remains to be seen.

No doubt, Caribbean and other Third World countries will have reason, once again, to see the professed principles of the old states, such as freedom and equality, disgraced by the old states themselves as they deal with other nations. But this should not discredit the principles themselves. Rather, it discredits the acts of unprincipled leaders and, through them, the nation itself. Furthermore, the struggle for equality has been just that, a struggle. The clash of interests and principles has and does characterize the domestic scene of the old states, as it does the new. But the long-term trend is clear: Many inequalities have been reduced; equality has spread.

EQUALITY AND EQUITY: TWO DIFFERENT CONCEPTS AND MEANINGS

The possibility of the continued forward march of equality would be a pleasant place to end a presidential address such as this: Hope for the future; the spread of more justice and equality for all within the national boundaries of our 160 or so states and even, with luck and effort, among them; and the rise of human dignity. That possibility, however, may not be highly probable.

The Meaning of Inequality.

One source of confusion and controversy arises over the meaning of the concept of equality and inequality. It is not the same, obviously, as the concept of equity or inequity. Inequality is basically a matter of statistical determination, while inequity is a matter of moral judgment. For example, a common element in all definitions of equality and inequality is the degree of similarity or difference between two or more individuals, groups, populations or other units which are compared with respect some specified characteristics. If the units being compared are the same, then they are equal. The more different they are, the greater the degree of inequality. Thus, the amount of inequality is the degree of heterogeneity in any distribution, maximum equality and inequality being two opposite poles of the same continuum which ranges from perfect similarity to maximum difference. Take income as an example. If everyone in a population has the same income, then there is complete equality of income. If incomes are different, the inequality increases as the average difference of everyone's income from everyone else's income increases.

Discourse about the facts of inequality, quite apart from the justice of it, becomes complicated, often seemingly contradictory, since there are so many empirical aspects of inequality one can measure. For example, we can speak of inequality of income within a whole society, such as within the entire Guyanese population. Or we can speak of the inequality of incomes comparing two or more populations, such as that between Guyana and Trinidad, or between two or more sub-populations within a single country, such as blacks and East Indians in Guyana.

In order to make statements about inequality, of course, explicit specification is needed in choosing the populations or groups to be compared. They could be based on gender, age, kinship connection, race and ethnic identity, religion, social class, nationality or region, to mention only a few of the frequently used social categories. The point is that some social unit must be specified within which or between which comparison is to be made and, usually, we expect some explanation as to why the comparison chosen is a meaningful one. Why, for example, should men be compared with women, young to old people, lower to middle and upper social classes, or members of different races with each other?

Furthermore, one must specify the variables on which units are to be compared. If we have a reason—usually some theory or interpretive framework—for comparing different races, for example, then on what characteristics should they be compared? Typically, social scientists have dealt with human rights and duties, such as civil or legal aspects (e.g., treatment by the courts), political aspects (e.g., voting), economic aspects (e.g., income, wealth, or occupation), social aspects (e.g., education), and cultural aspects (life styles and cultural identity).

Even getting the facts straight requires yet another complication. There are important differences among inequalities of (1) condition, (2) opportunity, (3) allocations or treatments, and (4) outcomes. For example, inequality in amount of education (a condition, such as the number of years of school completed) may be great even when there is equality of educational opportunity. In fact, since there are important differences in individual ability, motivation, and purpose, then equality of educational opportunity may imply inequality of educational achievement.

Also, allocation, that is treatments or inputs, can be distinguished from outcomes, that is the resulting condition from some process. For example, if we equate many of the inputs to a school, such as money for physical plant, books, and quality and quantity of teachers, we may find that outcomes such as achievement scores by the end of the twelfth year remain unequal between black and white students. Or to take a different example, through progressive income taxes we can take from high income people what we give to low income people through various welfare programs, thus creating more equal distributions of real income than would have occurred otherwise. In other words, we can treat people unequally in order to achieve the outcome of less inequality of conditions.

One can imagine a series of volumes in which the facts of inequalities of civil, political, economic, social, and cultural characteristics of different genders, ages, kin groups, race and ethnic groups, religious groups, social classes, and countries throughout the Caribbean were all described for several points in time up to the present according to the amount of inequality between or among them by measurements of conditions, opportunities, allocations, and outcomes. It is an enormous task. Yet it is what some Caribbean social researchers more or less have been working toward.[7] Such a comprehensive social mapping and analysis of various inequalities may be in the making. Whatever limited statements about inequality we are able to make in the meantime rest upon the availability of reliable data and the explicit organization and specification of (1) units to be compared, (2) some variables or goods that are distributed over them, and (3) some measure of the inequality of the variables or goods between or among the units. Such a program of research is essential for some current and future social policy decision-making.

The Meaning of Inequity

When we have finished the above program of research and described the inequalities that exist in Caribbean societies, we have not, even then, said anything whatsoever about the justice or fairness of equality or inequality. That is, we have said nothing about equity. The existence of inequality is a factual question. The existence of equity requires a value judgment, a judgment that in this case refers to whether or not a given equality or amount of inequality is fair or just.

Logically, it is a mistake to assume, as some writers have, that equality means equity and inequality means inequity. Actually, the relationship is problematic and requires some explicit logical justification before a scholarly or scientific judgment can be made. Thus, there are equalities *and* inequalities that are equitable, and there are equalities *and* inequalities that are inequitable. How can we decide when equalities or inequalities are fair and when they are not?

There are at least three basic ways that inequality or equality have been rationalized:

(1) Sacred. One common argument used to justify equality or inequality has been the sacred, that is appeal to "God's will" or "divine right."
(2) Natural law. Another argument is that equality or inequality is natural, that it is the consequence of the working out of nature, the result, for example, of some social evolutionary process, such as the survival of the fittest.
(3) Explicitly human constructions. Finally, a third argument is that some human viewpoint, rational argument, or theory justifies equality and inequality, such as, for example, a social contract between rulers and ruled or the idea of the "consent of the governed." This is not to say, or course, that appeals to the sacred and to nature are not also human constructions—humans created their gods and the "laws" of nature. But some rationalizations or appeals are admittedly and self-consciously human constructions, the deliberate "use of reason."

All three, for example, were used in the American Declaration of Independence. The first sentence contains an appeal both to nature and God:

> When in the Course of human Events it becomes necessary for one People to dissolve the Political Bands which have connected them with another, and to assume among the Powers of the Earth, the separate and equal Station to which the Laws of Nature and of Nature's God entitle them . . .

God is again invoked in the following passage: "We hold these Truths to be self-evident, that all Men are created equal, that they are endowed by their Creator with certain unalienable Rights. . . ."

And a consciously human construction can be seen in this phrase: ". . . driving their just Powers from the Consent of the Governed. . . ."

In the Caribbean today, as in most modern states, it is the explicitly human rationalizations of equality or inequality that interest us most, since these states are secular and stress such rationalizations. Thus, it is worthwhile to elaborate them. They include:

(a) The use of law, which is perhaps the most obvious of the ways in which distributive justice has been defined. Existing law is used and particular notions of distributive justice are codified into law to justify, challenge, or reshape existing social practice. Social legislation dealing with poor relief, social security, education, employment, and health, for example, have implications for equality or inequality and may be the means through which distributional reforms are made.

(b) The use of history, as Menno Boldt (1973) describes for the leaders of the Canadian Indian movement who justify their demands for more equality within Canadian society today in part by recourse to a conception of their traditional tribal past of equality. For old states, equality has been justified by an appeal to charter myths and documents as, for example, it was by John Porter (1965) in his analysis of the contrasting realities of inequalities of class and ethnicity in Canadian society.

(c) The use of logical deduction. Rawls (1971) posits "rational choosers" who are in an "original position" with a "veil of ignorance" covering their knowledge of where in a system of inequality they are or will be placed. By a series of deductions he then demonstrates how such rational choosers will construct a social contract by which inequality will be judged to be just or fair to the extent to which it redounds to the benefit of the most disadvantaged persons in the system. Presumably, some people who receive more than others will work harder and produce more and, thereby, increase the total wealth of the society making everyone better off than they would have been otherwise.

(d) The use of analysis of the collective judgments and behaviors of individuals, either (i) in laboratory or small group settings such as social psychological research on equity (Walster et al., 1978) or (ii) through survey research techniques designed to obtain interviews with specified populations (Bell and Robinson, 1978; Jasso and Rossi, 1977; Robinson and Bell 1978b).

The former has resulted in a convenient equation for thinking about equity.[8]

$$\frac{\text{Person or Group A's Rewards}}{\text{Pers or Grp A's Contributions}} \quad \text{as compared with} \quad \frac{\text{Person or Group B's Rewards}}{\text{Pers or Grp B's Contributions}}$$

When the ratios are the same, then equity exists. The more different they are, the more inequity exists. Clearly, the ratios can be the same, indicating perfect equity, even when there is great inequality of rewards as long as there is a comparable inequality of contributions. The equation simply says what many—if not most—persons in modern societies believe: There are unfair equalities and unfair inequalities and there are fair equalities and fair inequalities. It's as simple as that. Some people work harder or make more of a contribution than others and they ought to get more for it.

Corroborating evidence comes from survey research in which respondents have been asked to judge the fairness or unfairness of various inequalities or equalities between or among people, especially among different social classes and races. It is quite clear that ordinary people in their everyday lives do make such judgments. Moreover, not only do privileged persons judge some inequalities to be fair, but also many persons who are deprived do too. This is so partly because disadvantaged persons sometimes fear unwanted responsibilities; partly because they think they, too, may be privileged someday; and mostly because they judge many of the inequalities of reward within the stratification system of their society to be justly proportional to some sense of a person's—or class'— contribution to society.

In the sociological sense, it may be argued that the collective judgments of the members of a given society are the final recourse to which a question of social justice can be appealed and, of course, they can be empirically studied. Yet the type of argument defined below competes with it for definitiveness.

(e) The use of analysis of the functions of equality or inequality. A moral judgment of equality or inequality is here seemingly replaced by an empirical analysis of how a given amount of inequality functions for the society: Are certain equalities and inequalities necessary for society to survive or to get societal jobs done? Are they useful in producing benefits for people that would not exist without them? Of course, there is an underlying judgment that society ought to survive, that societal jobs ought to be done, or that certain effects ought to be judged as beneficial. But given these judgments, then it becomes a research task to determine what effects inequality produces for the society as a whole, for various subgroups of society, and for individuals. That is, how does inequality function? And for whom? In what ways?

The very fact that the social order is a complex network of interrelationships and patterns of routine behaviors that must be controlled and coordinated, guided and directed by some system of authority means that some kinds of inequalities of power are inevitable. The very fact that people must be motivated somehow to play a variety of social roles that vary in difficulty and burdensomeness without which society would be impossible implies that some degree of inequality of reward might be necessary. The very fact that most intrasocietal disputes and conflicts must be resolved without recourse to uncontrolled brute force if society is to survive suggests that some people must have the legitimate power to intervene and settle them. The very fact that modern society has a complex division of labor means that intricate social differentiation exists upon which invidious distinctions of power, prestige, property, participation, and privilege can be erected.

It is well known that privileged groups invent ideologies that justify their privileges and that such justifications may take the form of claims of functional necessities or benefits to society. The research task is, first, to explicate such ideologies when they exist, and perhaps formulate them when they don't. Second, to restate them as problematics. And third, to subject them to empirical test. How much inequality of what kind among what groups is *in fact* necessary for the survival of society or to get societal tasks accomplished? How much inequality is beneficial for society?

For Marx, of course, the meaning of inequality and inequity were central issues. His class analysis was both a description of the facts of inequality and an explanatory theory of them. And, brilliantly, he moved the concept of equity from purely moral to scientific discourse. His idea of surplus value, for example, permits a calculation of the amount of injustice heaped upon the working class by the capitalists. With the added concept of exploitation, calculable as the difference between wages and surplus value, he provided a justification for the proletariat to hate the bourgeoisie. What could be so starkly modern and emotionally inciting at the same time than a scientific demonstration of the existence of injustice? What better cause for righteous indignation and revolutionary action?

Thus, it is no wonder that it is Marx, although no less

Western than Adam Smith and hardly less a creature of the European Enlightenment than Condorcet, who has become a favorite intellectual forerunner of so many Third World intellectuals. Given the many unjust inequalities of colonialism, it is no wonder that many theorists of persistent poverty, unequal exchange among nations, and dependency have found modifications of Marx's ideas so serviceable.[9]

Yet Caribbean and other Third World scholars, obviously, have gone their own route—with, without, or beyond Marx—often formulating more sophisticated interpretations, more sensitive to the particular histories and conditions of their own countries. They have gone not one, but several different routes, in fact. Although, if I am correct in my thesis of the linked centrality of equality and social justice as the foundations of nationalism in the Caribbean and the influence on the Caribbean intellectual thought, then perhaps they lead to the same end. For example, M.G. Smith lays a solid groundwork of detailed, scientific analysis by his studies of the plural society which may be defined as congealed inequalities of culture, status, social organization, and race, as does Lloyd Braithwaite, working from a different theoretical tradition, in his study of social stratification in Trinidad; C.L.R. James in *The Black Jacobins* extends the range of concerns to include not only inequality but also injustice and rebellion; and Walter Rodney, Aimé Césaire and, especially, Frantz Fanon add the energizing forces of identity, consciousness, and the will to prevail as reactions to the oppressive domination of unjust inequalities. Many other examples could be given such as Lloyd Best and the Tapia Group in Trinidad, the histories of Eric Williams, and the Jamaican testament of Michael Manley.

ALIENATION AND THE LOSS OF LEGITIMACY?

Let us now consider the sources of legitimacy of a political regime because planned social change in the Caribbean, directly or indirectly, is largely and increasingly being carried out by the state. Political alienation and the withdrawal of legitimacy by the populace can result in the demise of the ruling group and erode the authority of the state itself. Many writers, including Lipset (1960) and Linz (1978), have discussed the importance of effectiveness and efficiency as cause of legitimacy. We can add equity or social justice to the equation:

Effectiveness + Efficiency + Equity = Legitimacy

and the obverse:

Ineffectiveness + Inefficiency + Inequity = Illegitimacy

By ineffectiveness, I refer to the inability of a political regime to perform the tasks that people regard as necessary to their survival, comfort, and self-realization. Many of the obstacles to effectiveness of course, come from the larger international world within which individual states find themselves inextricably and often interdependently linked. The power of multinational corporations, the uncontrolled — and often for a given state uncontrollable — rates of inflation, potentially hostile and aggressive neighboring states with territorial claims, the unstable prices of key commodities on the world markets, growing debts, crippling racial and cultural conflict, and in the Caribbean, of course, as Errol Barrow said at the 1980 Caribbean Studies Association conference in Curaçao, the concept of limited sovereignty for

Caribbean states held by some U.S. leaders (and, therefore, American violation of it)—these and similar forces erode the ability of Caribbean governments to perform effectively. But beyond that are forces of the will and the organizational expertise to get the jobs done—ordinary things like delivering the mail, repairing the roads, keeping the telephone system working and the electricity on. Not to mention the more difficult things like providing jobs, health care, unemployment insurance, old age pensions, and housing; protecting life and limb; maintaining order, and the other aspects of life modern citizens have been taught to expect of government. More and more, in country after country, the situation seems out of control, the burdens of expectation and responsibility seem beyond the capacities of government to carry. Polities become overloaded. Increasingly expected to do everything, political regimes frequently do some thing poorly. Alienation toward the state grows; the legitimacy of the state erodes.

The problem is compounded by the growing loss of efficiency, in part as a result of increasing scale beyond capacity for communication, control, and the number of available trained personnel. Nearly everywhere, in both the new and old states, government continues to grow in size absolutely and relatively: as a proportion of GNP, as a percentage of all workers, and as a separate class with its own emergent interests. In some Caribbean states government and public sector spending may now have reached 50 percent of GNP. Outmoded organizational forms add to the dreadful waste which is multiplied by corruption. The confidence, knowledge, ability, and motivation to produce and maintain the efficient organizational instruments—the tools of human action—that are needed to inspire the trust and faith of the people seem in short supply.

But no regime, no matter how effective and efficient, can secure its legitimacy if it is perceived as unjust. Thus, many of the political regimes of the new states, already struggling to achieve or to maintain effective and efficient functioning, must simultaneously cope with their people's expanded expectations for social justice. The very meaning of their sovereignty, as we have seen, is tied to the promise of social justice. Furthermore, given the inequalities of colonialism and the ideology of equality available in Western political thought, social justice meant equality. So much was this true that the rhetoric by which political independence was defended by nationalist elites in the British Caribbean, for example, was often entirely in terms of equalities (which were assumed to be fair) and inequalities (which were assumed to be unfair) and no explicit mention of justice or fairness may have been made whatsoever, except insofar as the latter were intended as implicit synonyms for equality. Thus, Caribbean governments face the continued demand for more equality on the part of some deprived citizens who have been told that equality means more for them and who believe it to be just. And such people may withdraw their support as quickly from a regime that permits a privileged "shirt-jac," bureaucratic, state elite to arise as from one that permits the continuation of privileges of a suit-and-tie, capitalist, entrepreneurial class. Furthermore, in the political realm the principle of equality of participation is violated when elections are rigged, when they are no longer free and fair. A basic claim to legitimacy is thereby lost.

The situation in the new states of the Caribbean today seems to include the following:

(1) Attitudes toward political independence are no longer problematic. Persons who opposed it, fairly numerous even in the early 1960s, have left the countries, died, withdrawn from active political life, or converted to the view that political independence is desirable. This is so despite the fact that the underlying principle of self-determination does not necessarily imply political inde-

pendence. Rather, it means the right of a people to choose their political status, be it independence, self-government within a protective agreement with another country, free associative status, or full integration with another political entity (Alexander and Friedlander, 1980).

(2) Civil and political equalities are generally judged to be fair, but violations of implementation are alleged, for example, in Guyana and elsewhere where charges of rigged elections and bogus voting are widespread. A growing sense of injustice is thereby promoted.

(3) Equality of opportunity in economic life is nearly everywhere considered to be fair, and in social policy it is often the aim. In reality wide inequalities of economic opportunity are the norm.

(4) Equality of citizenship with citizens of other countries largely has been achieved in its psychological and political dimensions. It is, of course, universally considered just.

(5) The battle for agreement that social and cultural equality, both of opportunity and condition, is fair seems to be nearly over. This is not to say that social and cultural equality has been achieved. Rather, some consensus about what is fair has emerged. Few people in the Caribbean new states today will argue that there should be ascribed social barriers separating people on the basis of race or class. Moreover, Anglo-European life styles and identities, so dominant during colonial times in the former British Caribbean, have been largely replaced by local variants of Caribbean creole culture. The African heritage, once despised, now receives wide respect and recognition.

(6) Despite the rhetoric of equality that ushered in the new states in the Caribbean, there still exists gross internal inequalities of condition in the economic sphere, in employment, occupation, income, and wealth. Although some inequalities are holdovers from the past, some are newly created as the new middle class of bureaucrats,

technocrats, politicians and civil servants connected with the state apparatus has grown and prospered. Some members of society, especially segments of the lower racial and social-economic classes and some far left intellectuals and leaders, judge the privileges of the new middle class as unjust. Some of these people feel alienation and rage.

(7) Yet alienation and rage toward Caribbean political regimes comes also from the relatively privileged classes as well, especially from the entrepreneurial class, some professionals, some skilled workers, and even from some members of the new state elite. Their privileges in their judgment have been unfairly jeopardized. They are, or so they believe, the victims of injustice, unfair efforts to create equality at their expense or to reward them with less than they deserve. They are joined in their judgment that when it comes to income or wealth, inequality is fair by some members of all social classes and racial groups, probably a majority of people. Thus, political regimes that simply equate social justice with equality or income and wealth across the board may face a sudden setback. And their opponents will be speaking the rhetoric of social justice (fair inequalities), though not the rhetoric of equality of condition. And finally:

(8) Conflict over how much of a role the state should play in the economy has replaced the pre-independence cleavage between pro and con attitudes toward political independence as the major focus of political struggle. Although nearly all Caribbean people may agree that the foreign transnational ox should be gored to their individual and collective national advantage, they vehemently disagree on how much control, regulation, or ownership the state should have over those enterprises in which the national bourgeoisie have major interests. In Jamaica, for example, this question recently completely polarized political activity and the aims of the two major political parties, the People's National Party having pushed for more state

control and ownership and the Jamaica Labour Party having wanted a more limited role for government.

There are dilemmas here, a series of interrelated contradictions. Equality of opportunity is incompatible with some aspects of equality of condition. The demand for justice defined as more equality continues in some parts of the population, while at the same time the demand for justice defined as some degree of inequality (a reward commensurate with skill, talent, extraordinary performance, risk taking, investment in training, or whatever) is strident among some groups, such as entrepeneurial groups in Jamaica. De facto inequality as seen in the rising bureaucratic and state elite occurs in the face of continued use of the idea of equality as justice to validate the very creation and expansion of the state apparatus that itself produces the privileges of the bureaucratic and state elite.

Simple interest theory—that deprived groups want equality and privileged groups want inequality because each group benefits the most that way—does not explain all of the variance of who defines social justice as equality or inequality. This is so because a number of other variables can intervene in the relationship, such as education (which is correlated with economic privilege but can lead to egalitarian values), other values (such as achievement and success, which are compatible with many kinds of inequalities), and fears of responsibilities, religious and other beliefs (Lane, 1962; Robinson and Bell, 1978b).

CONCLUSION

If we have reached the zenith of the age of the nation-state, perhaps we should begin to expect that we may soon arrive at its nadir. Many writers have predicted the demise of the nation-state, one of the latest being Alvin Toffler (1980: 30). The usual threats to the sovereignty of the state that are proposed are supranational organizations of one kind or another, such as larger regional groupings, transnational corporations, and world institutions on the one hand, or fragmenting smaller groups defined by race, ethnicity, or religion on the other.

In this article I suggest an additional source of threat to the state. Along with the oftcited causes of the loss of legitimacy of a political regime represented by its ineffectiveness and inefficiency, I stress its inequity. Feelings of inequity not only could topple a regime, but they could also erode the legitimacy of the state itself if a regime remained in power by force or fraud and if the state became the manager of most of economic and social life.

The injustices of which I speak are those involving certain equalities and inequalities. Although the assertion that some inequalities, especially of income and wealth, are fair may give solace to the privileged, it also may be an unwelcome truth that political leaders should take seriously if they want to prevent alienation and promote their own legitimacy.

The Caribbean is today a battle field of an intense clash of ideologies, a microcosm of world struggle. Western-style party democracies exist alongside dictatorships of the left and of the right. Capitalist, democratic socialist, and communist ideologies struggle to capture the future. But the debate, as I understand it, often is beside the point. Forgotten is the fact that there may be more variation from a global perspective within than between regimes characterized by the labels these various dogmas have generated. For example, Yugoslavia has more political liberties and popular sovereignty than some other communist countries such as the Soviet Union or Albania. Capitalist Canada is more politically democratic than capitalist Portugal or Honduras. Throughout the

1960s, communist Yugoslavia was more democratic than capitalist countries such as Taiwan and Spain. Socialist countries of Scandinavia score higher on political democracy than a number of capitalist nations (Bollen, 1978). And official Soviet policy long ago denounced "equality mongering."

Perhaps we should ignore the labels and look at the facts of public liberties, political participation, and, as has been the central theme of this study, social justice as it is manifested in various fair equalities and inequalities. Thus, there is a research agenda underlying this article, an agenda that must be carried out before the performance of the new national leaders and the alternative futures they offer can be adequately assessed. It includes, first, the mapping of the various equalities and inequalities within and among Caribbean societies, and, second, an appraisal, perhaps by some of the procedures purposed here, of their fairness.

Given the central importance of equality and social justice to the creation and meaning of the new Caribbean states and to the continuing legitimacy of their political regimes, economic organizations, social arrangements, and cultural orientations, then such a research agenda seems imperative. Furthermore, such a research agenda—obviously already underway as I have said—is of importance to the current efforts to reduce international inequalities by creating a new international economic order; its results, for example, inform the North-South dialogue. And, perhaps just as urgently needed, is such research from the viewpoints of the new states in order to cross-fertilize that in the old states where, it should not be forgotten, the struggle to control the definitions of what inequalities are fair goes on in the face of many forces dedicated to the maintenance of old inequalities and the creation of new ones.

In conclusion, if my effort to link nationalism, equality, and social justice in the new states with similar phenomena in the old states and with Western traditions is read as mere ethnocentrism, then I have not been properly understood. If Western conceptions and values have been used and abused by European colonial powers to perpetuate conditions of inferiority and infelicity, then it is not the values that should be rejected but their abuse. If a concern with the social justice of inequality is a Western tradition, then it has co-existed, often been dominated by, and struggled over the centuries with a no less Western tradition of social injustice. For example, there may be less hypocrisy in Western colonialism than Césaire or Fanon would have us believe: conquest, domination, plunder, superiority were the unmasked aims, values, and beliefs of many would-be imperial masters. Questioning the justice of existing inequalities has seldom been an endearing quality in the eyes of any Western ruling elite. Controversy over social justice arises in Western history again and again. And it is not that Western ideals have universal validity. It is, rather, that some Western ideals may be one expression of some values that do have universal validity. The search for that validity, however, transcends any particular past of any particular peoples and will be defined, eventually, by its future destination toward which we have all been advanced by the works of many scholars, most recently by Caribbean and other Third World scholars.[10]

EPILOGUE – 1990

It has been ten years since this paper was written. Today, there are over 100 new states, and, since 1980, three additional new states in the Caribbean, Belize and Antigua-and-Barbuda which became independent in 1981 and St. Kitts-Nevis in 1983. Thus, the transition to nationhood has continued. Even fewer colonies remain from which to form additional independent states than in 1980, so the process must be coming to an end—unless, of course, existing states begin to break-up into smaller units. Some evidence exists that such a break-up is a possibility, though, no doubt, unlikely to occur on a large scale. Yet the dramatic fragmentation of Soviet-dominated Eastern Europe and the reassertion of national sovereignty in Hungary, Poland, Czechoslovakia, Romania, Bulgaria, and East Germany certainly can be viewed as a resurgence of the global democratic revolution. Although these countries had been politically independent states de jure, they had been, as we all know, de facto more or less under the hegemony of the Soviet Union. Moreover, their example, if followed by subregional peoples within the borders of the Soviet Union, may presage a fourth wave of new state creation, already visible in Lithuania and the other Baltic states.

The present thaw in the cold war, if it continues—and there is no reason why it should not, means a totally different international environment. As I write, the Soviet Union is itself undergoing a democratic transition, and the United States, after the humiliating Iran-Contra scandal and the misguided and unnecessary invasion of Grenada in 1983 (Bell, 1986), will have little excuse to support corrupt and antidemocratic armies abroad in the name of fighting Communism, as it has done in El Salvador, Honduras, Guatemala, and, before the capture of Manuel Antonio Noriega, in Panama. Democracies, as my colleague Bruce Russett points out, do not fight each other.

The "peace dividend" could be enormous, not only for the Soviets and Americans, but also for the countries of the Third World. Instead of weapons, proxy wars, and distrust, we can hope for cooperation, mutual help, and coordinated development. The creation of a pan-Caribbean community to coordinate and control economic relations with the rest of the world may be the way to maximize both Caribbean contributions to and benefits from international trade and exchange. But such an image of the future is only one among many. What are the alternative possibilities? How can cooperation, human rights, democratic decision-making, social justice, economic and social well-being, mutual respect, and cultural dignity be secured? How can the new Caribbean states achieve the meaning and purpose of their nationhood? The answer may be to continue the drive for economic and social development along with the struggle for democracy and equity, fostering a continuing debate as social change occurs about which equalities and inequalities are fair and which are unfair.

NOTES

*This is a revised version of a presidential address delivered at the annual conference of the Caribbean Studies Association in Curaçao, Netherlands Antilles, May 7–10, 1980. I wish to thank Angel Calderón Cruz, Locksley Edmondson, and René Römer for their comments on an earlier version of this address.
1. One misunderstanding of our work is the erroneous belief that we only studied leaders. We also studied students and slum dwellers in Jamaica and sugar workers in Antigua. We did, however, concentrate much of our effort on elites because of their importance for the decision-making and design perspective we adopted.
2. See Bell (1964), Bell (1967), Bell and Oxaal (1964), Duke (1963), Mau (1968), Moskos (1967), and Murch (1971).
3. The question of the form of government is related in that there is evidence to show that countries with democratic regimes, regardless of level of economic development, have less internal income inequality than do undemocratic countries (Weede, 1980). But democracy does not need this justification because it is, of course, its own reward: people who manage to establish and maintain it enjoy both public liberties and the periodic opportunity to throw rascal rulers out.

4. This is so, for example, for a percentage as it moves from 0 which is perfect equality (no one has any of a good), to 50 which is maximum inequality (half have some and half have none), to 100 which is perfect equality again (everyone has the good). For empirical support for the curvilinear relationship between economic development and income inequality, see Ahluwalia (1976), Chenery and Syrquin (1975), Paukert (1973), and Weede (1980). The question, however, of the definition of maximum inequality is subject to alternative interpretations depending on the type of variable being considered (Blau, 1977).
5. This is not to say that the issue of racial inequality has been dealt with in a more effective way in the United States than in the Caribbean. Just the opposite is the case. Many Caribbean countries have moved toward reducing racial inequalities more quickly and with less violence than has the United States.
6. For review of the revolution in civil rights in the United States, see Berger (1968) and Congressional Quarterly Service (1967).
7. My work and that of my associates, of course, has prominently included the topic of inequality. Other Caribbean scholars whose work bears on the topic, to mention just a few, include Fuat M. Andic, George L. Beckford, Compton Bourne, Lloyd Braithwaite, Malcolm Cross, George Cumper, Locksley Edmondson, Norman Girvan, J.E. Greene, Basil Ince, Vaughan Lewis, Louis Lindsay, G.E. Mills, M.G. Smith, and Carl Stone.
8. For a more complicated equation which allows for negative numbers, e.g., punishments as well as rewards, see Walster et al. (1978).
9. For example, see Beckford (1972); Cardoso and Faletto (1979); Dos Santos (1970); Frank (1967); Girvan (1973); Moran (1974); and Sunkel (1973).
10. Of course, in this short article I have barely scratched the surface of the growing body of work by scholars of the Caribbean new states and said little or nothing about much of the excellent and important work of writers from other areas of the Caribbean.

REFERENCES

Agee, Philip. 1975. *Caribbean Contact* (June).
Ahluwalia, Montek S. 1976. "Income distribution and development: Some stylized facts," *American Economic Review* 66 (May): 128-135.
Alexander, Yonah and Robert A. Friedlander (eds.). 1980. *Self-Determination: National, Regional and Global Dimensions*. Boulder, CO: Westview.
Alger, Janet Merrill. 1972. "The Sociology of the American Revolution," Ph.D. Dissertation, Yale University.
Beckford, George L. 1972. *Persistent Poverty: Underdevelopment in Plantation Economies of the Third World*. New York: Oxford University Press.
Bell, Wendell. 1964. *Jamaican Leaders: Political Attitudes in a New Nation*. Berkeley and Los Angeles, CA: University of California Press.
_____ (ed.). 1967. *The Democratic Revolution in the West Indies: Studies in Nationalism, Leadership, and the Belief in Progress*. Cambridge, MA: Schenkman.
_____. 1977. "Inequality in independent Jamaica: A preliminary appraisal of elite performance." *Revista/Review Interamericana* 7 (Summer): 294-308.
_____. 1986. "The invasion of Grenada: A note on false prophecy." *Yale Review* 75 (Summer): 564-586.
Bell, Wendell and Ivar Oxaal. 1964. *Decisions of Nationhood: Political and Social Development in the British Caribbean*. Denver, CO: Social Science Foundation, University of Denver.
Bell, Wendell and Robert V. Robinson. 1978. "An index of evaluated equality: Measuring conceptions of social justice in England and the United States." Pp. 235-270 in Richard F. Tomasson (ed.), *Comparative Studies in Sociology*, Vol. I. Greenwich, CT: JAI Press.
Bell, Wendell and David L. Stevenson. 1979. "Attitudes toward social equality in independent Jamaica: Twelve years after nationhood." *Comparative Political Studies* 11 (January): 499-532.

Berger, Morroe. 1968. *Equality by Statute: The Revolution in Civil Rights*, rev. ed. Garden City, NY: Doubleday, Anchor.

Blau, Peter M. 1977. *Inequality and Heterogeneity*. New York: Free Press.

Boldt, Menno. 1973. "Indian Leaders in Canada: Attitudes Toward Equality, Identity and Political Status," Ph.D. Dissertation, Yale University.

Bollen, Kenneth A. 1978. "Issues in the comparative measurement of political democracy." *American Sociological Review* 45 (June): 370–390.

Cardoso, Fernando H. and Enzo Faletto. 1979. *Dependency and Development in Latin America*. Berkeley, CA: University of California Press.

Chenery, Hallis and Moises Syrquin. 1975. *Patterns of Development 1950–1970*. London: Oxford University Press.

Congressional Quarterly Service. 1967. *Revolution in Civil Rights*. Washington, D.C.

Crile, George. 1974. "Our man in Jamaica." *Harper's* (October): 87–96.

Dos Santos, Theotonio. 1970. "The structure of dependence." *American Economic Review* 60 (May): 231–236.

Duke, James T. 1963. "Equalitarianism Among Emergent Elites in a New Nation." Ph.D. Dissertation, University of California, Los Angeles.

Frank, Andre Gunder. 1967. *Capitalism and Underdevelopment in Latin America: Historical Studies of Chile and Brazil*. New York: Monthly Review Press.

Girvan, Norman. 1973. "The development of dependency economics in the Caribbean and Latin America: Review and comparison." *Social and Economic Studies* 22 (March): 1–33.

Hayes, Carlton J.H. 1950. *The Historical Evolution of Modern Nationalism*. New York: Macmillan.

Jasso, Guillermina and Peter H. Rossi. 1977. "Distributive justice and earned income." *American Sociological Review* 42 (August): 639–651.

Kohn, Hans. 1957. *American Nationalism*. New York: Macmillan.

_____. 1965. *Nationalism: Its Meaning and History*, rev. ed. Princeton, NJ: Princeton University Press.
Lane, Robert E. 1962. *Political Ideology*. New York: Free Press.
Linz, Juan J. 1978. "Crisis, breakdown, and reequilibration," Vol. 1 of Juan J. Linz and Alfred Stepan (eds.), *The Breakdown of Democratic Regimes*. Baltimore, MD: Johns Hopkins University Press.
Lipset, Seymour Martin. 1960. *Political Man*. Garden City, NY: Doubleday.
_____. 1963. *The First New Nation*. New York: Basic Books.
Manchester, William. 1975. *The Glory and the Dream*, Vol. II. Boston: Little, Brown.
Mau, James. A. 1968. *Social Change and Images of the Future*. Cambridge, MA: Schenkman.
Moran, Theodore H. 1974. *Multinational Corporations and the Politics of Dependence: Copper in Chile*. Princeton, NJ: Princeton University Press.
Moskos, Charles C. Jr. 1967. *The Sociology of Political Independence: A Study of Nationalist Attitudes Among West Indian Leaders*. Cambridge, MA: Schenkman.
Murch, Arvin W. 1971. *Black Frenchmen: The Political Integration of the French Antilles*. Cambridge, MA: Schenkman.
Palmer, R. R. 1959 abd 1965. *The Age of the Democratic Revolution: A Political History of Europe and America, 1760–1800*. Vol. I, "The Challenge," and Vol. II, "The Struggle." Princeton, NJ: Princeton University Press.
Paukert, Felix. 1973. "Income levels at different levels of development: A survey of evidence." *International Labour Review* 108 (August–September): 97–125.
Porter, John. 1965. *The Vertical Mosaic*. Toronto, Canada: University of Toronto Press.
Rawls, John. 1971. *A Theory of Justice*. Cambridge, MA: Belknap Press of Harvard.
Robinson, Robert V. and Wendell Bell. 1978a. "Attitudes towards political independence in Jamaica after twelve years of nationhood." *British Journal of Sociology* 29 (June): 208–233.
_____. 1978b. "Equality, success, and social justice in England the

United States." *American Sociological Review* 43 (April): 125–143.
Sunkel, Osvaldo. 1973. "Transnational capitalism and national disintegration in Latin America." *Social and Economic Studies* 22 (March): 132–176.
Toffler, Alvin. 1980. *The Third Wave*. New York: William Morrow.
Walster, Elaine, G. William Walster, and Ellen Berscheid. 1978. *Equity: Theory and Research*. Boston: Allyn and Bacon.
Weede, Erich. 1980. "Beyond Misspecification in Sociological Analyses of Income Inequality," *American Sociological Review* 45 (June): 497–501.

BRIEF BIOGRAPHY

NAME	Wendell Bell
DATE OF BIRTH	September 27 1924
ACADEMIC DEGREES	Ph.D. University of California, Los Angeles, 1952
	M.A. California State University, Fresno, 1951
	B.A. California State University, Fresno, 1948
ACADEMIC AFFILIATIONS	Member of the Faculty of UCLA, Northwestern University, and Stanford University
	Professor of Yale since 1963 – Present Chairman of the Sociology Department
	Chairman and Director of Undergraduate Studies at Yale University

BOOKS

Social Area Analysis 1955

Decisions of Nationhood: Political and Social Development in the British Caribbean (1964)

Public Leadership (1961)

The Sociology of the Future (1971)

The Democratic Revolution in the West Indies, 1967

Ethnicity and Nation Building (1974)

SELECTED ARTICLES

"Futuro," *Enciclopedia delle Scienze Sociale* Roma Italia, 1990 (in Italian)

"The Rise of Futures Thinking in the New States: The Decisions of Nationhood," in H.F. Didsbury, Jr. (ed.)

"The Future: Opportunity Not Destiny, Bethesda, MD: World Future Society, 1989

"An Epistemology for the Futures Field, *Futures* 21, (2) (April, 1989)

"What is a Preferable Future? How Do We Know?" in Jim Dator and Maria Guido Roulstone (eds.)

"Who Cares? And How? Futures of caring Societies" Honolulu, HI: University of Hawaii at Manoa, 1988

"Is the Futures Field an Art Form or Can It Become a Science?" *Futures Research Quarterly*, 1987

OTHER INFORMATION	Member of Program of African Studies Yale University
	Naval Aviator During World War II
	Current Interests: Sociology of The Future

The US and the Caribbean: Issues of Economics and Security

VAUGHAN A. LEWIS

The independence of the larger British Caribbean states Trinidad and Tobago and Jamaica, took place at a time (August 1962) of intense American concern and activity in the Caribbean, dominated by the United States' difficulties with the new revolutionary regime of Cuba. The government of the United States sought to isolate Cuba from the other countries of Latin America and the Caribbean; and to ensure that those states would not be affected by any spread of communism and Soviet influence. This was the rationale for the American intervention in the Dominican Republic in 1965.

The United States expected, and her expectation was largely met, that the new Caribbean states that achieved full sovereignty during this period, would follow the guidelines about inhibition of communist influence laid down by herself in and for the Inter-American system. And from the point of view of these Caribbean states, the active demonstration of this requirement was the determined exercise of American influence in the resolution of the racial/political dispute in Guyana (then British Guiana) during the first half of the 1960s. The United States government was at that time concerned to ensure that any regime taking the country into independence would give allegiance to the US Inter-American system position.

The eventual mode of resolution of the Guyana issue, indicates an important fact of Caribbean domestic politics: the element of voluntary cooperation and subordination in relations with the United States, borne in part of the socialization of most of the political elite of the period into pre- and post-war ideologies of anti-communism and anti-Stalinism. But it indicated also, at the level of the external relations the changing nature of hegemonic relationships in the Caribbean: the *de facto* cession by the British, of responsibility for the maintenance of order and regional security for what had been up to then their segment of the Western Hemisphere. This cession to the United States paralleled the British decision to reorganize the international economic relationships (and by implication political relationships) of the United Kingdom, through her application for entry into the European Economic Community (EEC). This decision was in turn perceived by the new Caribbean states as having the potential for threatening their own economic viability; for it would in effect remove the economic underpinning of the old imperial (hegemonic) relationship.

For the Caribbean, these processes in fact reflected the gradual domination by North America of the Caribbean economic staples (export commodities producing foreign exchange)—bauxite, tourism. (We might note too, the American purchase of the small British petroleum facilities in Trinidad.) The expansion of tourism, particularly in Jamaica, was itself partly a consequence of the United States' difficulties with Cuba and the virtual ending of the US-Cuba trade and communication. We might note also that the United States opposed the initial United Kingdom/EEC proposals for a set of reciprocal relationships in trade and investment—the so-called reverse preferences—between the Caribbean and the Community. But this was done not so much with the possible volumes of Caribbean trade and investment in mind, but with the view that it would set a negative example for global trading arrangements; the United States being concerned to ensure that there was no increase in trade discrimination against herself. This is, however, an early example of the American tendency to safeguard her Caribbean and Latin American interests, and to treat them as exemplary in the context of the patterns of global arrangements which she wished to see exist.

Nonetheless, into the first half of the 1970s, a general stabilization of these new Caribbean states' relationships appeared to have been arrived at, satisfactory to all. The states (with the exception of Guyana for special reasons) joined and accepted the obligations of the Inter-American system—the OAS; their traditional international economic relationships were regularized in the Lomé Convention within which were included new arrangements for economic and technical aid. And within the sub-region itself, some stability was apparently given to country-to-country relations, and to the possible trends in their foreign policies, through the attempt to institutionalize the harmonization of foreign policy decision-making within the Caribbean Community (CARICOM).

In general, the Caribbean countries, and in particular Jamaica and Guyana were deemed to have benefitted from the isolation of Cuba. North American investment in tourism and bauxite in Jamaica secured continuously high rates of economic growth. Jamaica in turn had accepted all the American institutional terms for foreign investment: the Hickenlooper amendment, Overseas Private Investment Corporation (OPIC) and International Centre for Settlement of Investment Disputes (ICSID) (within the World Bank system). The new regime in Guyana under Forbes Burnham set out to reap the financial rewards of fealty to the United States hemispheric line after its independence, and quickly dismantled previous economic arrangements with Cuba established by the government of Cheddi Jagan. Many of these independent Caribbean states now came to be considered "middle income countries" with respect to the international aid institutions; thereby disqualifying themselves from receipt of "soft" loans.

In this overall appearance of stabilization in the late 1960s and early 1970s, there were one or two dark clouds — intimations of the potential for disorder. Domestic economic difficulties after 1965 culminated in a youth-cum-military rebellion in Trinidad in 1970. Trinidad's oil production had entered a period of persistent decline, the government had begun to experience foreign exchange difficulties, and difficulties in raising loans on external markets on reasonable conditions; the government was increasingly incapable of satisfying the demands for employment of a youth population which had been the recipient of a substantially expanded educational program; and in the face of all this the government's own sense of self-confidence began to decline. In Jamaica too, the pace of economic growth, however impressive, was not capable of satisfying the requirements of those placing themselves on the job market. Increasing social discontent found expression in the brief spell of rioting in 1968 (the Rodney riots). This the government was able to subdue, but it thenceforth increasingly displayed a degree of nervousness towards its own population.

The quick muting of these uprisings in the two leading countries of the sub-region, was accompanied by a tendency on the part of the governments to increase their emphasis and dependence on instruments of security. The political directorate was inclined to attribute the disturbances not to the development of broad social discontent in their communities, but to small fringes of the intelligentsia and other attracted to Marxism and other radical ideologies. Conspiratorial explanations were evident in, for example, the Report of the commission of inquiry established in Trinidad during the 1960s; and in the speeches and activities of members of the Jamaican government. American diplomacy also, was not unaffected, as is evident from the report prepared by Ambassador Milton Barrall for the United States Department. In general, however, the governments felt themselves capable of maintaining local stability.

Finally, as far as the rest of the colonial Caribbean was concerned, the dominant American problem of securing proper arrangements for regional order and security was ensured by linking the territories in these areas (defense and foreign relations) to the metropolitan centers. For the territories in the British Caribbean the institution of Associated Statehood was devised. Such arrangements allowed for swift intervention in the event of local disorder.

This appearance of general stability seems dramatically changed today. In the American view, a major crisis appears to exist in the archipelago Caribbean (the West Indies). There is a perception of Cuban "expansionism," and the making of diplomatic "gains" by that country in both the large and the small states. There is a perception of danger implicit in the development of communication and relationships between the hitherto institutionally separated sub-regions of the West Indies and Central America, suggested in relationships between Grenada, Cuba, Jamaica (before the recent general election) and Nicaragua. The recent election in Jamaica has been interpreted as a victory against "Marxism" and "radicalism." For America policy-makers and corporate interests, the central concern has been the effect of the assumed radicalization of Caribbean internal and external policy on American interests, in which are included American security interests, in the area.

UNITED STATES INTERESTS: A SUMMARY

The United States considers the area in general as an important security zone, along with Central America; and considers instability there as threatening to her own security, where such instability is likely to serve as a magnet for non-hemispheric (that is, Communist) intervention or interference. While it is the case that other areas of the globe are perhaps given a greater day-to-day significance in strategic terms, this zone represents the fundamental underpinning, as part of the geographically proximate hemisphere, of the American system of security arrangements. Hence the term "America's backyard," frequently is used to describe it. Since the revolutionary regime of Cuba is seen as a local proxy for the global socialist system, a Cuban presence in any country is now automatically perceived as "outside intervention." In American perceptions, some administrations and congressional leaders distinguish between a Cuban military presence (as did Kissinger in 1976) which is considered unacceptable, and a Cuban technical assistance and diplomatic presence. Others however hold that there is no *a priori* difference between the two kinds of presences, and that the security implications of each need to be examined on a case by case basis.

The Caribbean Sea, linking the West Indies and Central America, is seen as the American Mediterranean whose security constitutes a part of the general area of American hemisperic security. The Caribbean Sea remains an important transit route for trade to and from the United States, petroleum, for example, being an especially important economic and strategic commodity transported therein. The Caribbean thus becomes linked with the Panama Canal which still retains important economic and strategic interest for the United States and her allies. For an important American hemispheric economic and security partner, Venezuela, the passages through the Caribbean islands constitute her gateway to the North Atlantic.

The United States is concerned in this era, to ensure the uninterrupted continuation of trade in Caribbean mineral resources, in particular bauxite. This requirement becomes linked to the questions of local policy on the terms of foreign investment, and policy relating to the diversification of Caribbean mineral exports. It is today increasingly concerned with the effects within the US itself, of the movement—both legal and illegal—of Caribbean peoples to America as well as with the illegal movement of drugs from and through the Caribbean states. These last two areas of interest induce in turn a concern with the economic and institutional weaknesses in the structure of Caribbean political and social systems.

The American interests in these varieties of areas give rise, given the over-riding US concern with security, to what appears to be an American perception of a general incapacity on the part of the regimes of the islands, either because of smallness and/or weakness, to hold autonomous positions in relationships deemed actually or potentially hostile to the United States. In that context, the American response is to react negatively and preemptively—to act "in anticipation" so to speak, of the development of any such relationships. Her perception of the recent experience of Jamaica (seen as nearly having slipped away into the communist camp) reinforces this orientation. In the Caribbean the United States perceives, then, a potential vacuum, in the traditional international relations sense.

But what the United States policy makers suddenly see as a crisis of regional security—specifically of Cuban communist expansion into a weak area—in the short time perspective of American decision-making, can more usefully be seen (and many in the Caribbean prefer to see) as a slowly developing crisis of economic and social (dis)organization implicit in the economic and social development strategies of the 1960s, and maturing at the present time; a crisis not susceptible to military/security solutions, or solutions designed essentially to inhibit the normalization of relations between the Caribbean states and Cuba.

Of course, the mere fact that the United States arrives at the situation of defining a period as one of crisis in security terms, or a geographical area as a crisis zone, becomes, or ought to become a factor and an input in the structure of Caribbean decision-making. It was perhaps one of the errors of the Manley administration in Jamaica that it failed to assess in time, and to attribute sufficient significance to, the American definition of its policy as having the potential of creating a security crisis for the United States, however invalid such a definition might have been.

SOCIAL CRISIS AND POLITICAL ORIENTATION

Jamaica experienced fairly rapid economic growth in the 1960s, fuelled by substantial foreign investment in the bauxite and tourism industries, and by investment in manufacturing partly for the country's domestic market, on the basis of incentives to both local and foreign investors, provided by the government. As a result, there was also an expansion of the commercial and services sectors, and an expansion of the range of indigenous skills appropriate to the degree of economic expansion. On the other hand, during the period, the country's range of agricultural exports, relatively diversified (bananas, sugar, citrus, tobacco, coffee) began to experience for the most part, fairly persistent declines. In spite of the

UNITED STATES DOMINANCE 55

existence of strong trade unions, wages in the agricultural sector lagged (as is not uncommon) behind those in the new industrial and service sectors.

Fairly rapid population growth, combined with improvements in health and welfare, when added to these phenomena, resulted in a situation of large resources of labor which the industrial sector was incapable of absorbing, in spite of the rapid rates of growth. Large pockets of unemployed, in particular unemployed youth, became visible; a visibility exacerbated by the fact of substantial shifts of population from rural areas to the urban centers experiencing economic growth. Toward the end of the 1960s the political elites were becoming uncomfortably aware that these large pockets of unemployed, many functionally illiterate, and perhaps unemployable individuals, could provide dangerous political fodder.

The Caribbean political elite is particularly sensitive to the question of large scale unemployment and its possible political effects, since for the most part that elite derives from the trade union movement which entered political office when the British conceded universal adult suffrage. This political elite gained office on the specific promise to the working class that they could and would provide this class with the economic inheritance from which it had previously been deprived by colonialism and the local landed oligarchy which dominated the economic systems of the Caribbean territories. With the maturing of the investment process in bauxite and tourism in Jamaica by the beginning of the 1970s, the political directorate of that country now had to seek other, or additional, means for coping with the surge in unemployment, to meet the expectations of the working class.

The relatively minor riots in Jamaica in 1968 (the Rodney riots), induced the government to increase its emphasis on security measures, as it sought to maintain the degree of social and political stability deemed necessary for the attraction of new foreign investment. But this had the domestic consequence of an increasing sense of social crisis for which new solutions had to be sought. This was the context of the entry into office of the People's National Party government of Michael Manley in 1972, the party having run its campaign in the two-party competitive system of Jamaica, on the basis of a promise of modernization of the economic system in such a manner as to maintain economic growth while ensuring the unemployed masses their legitimate economic and social rights.

The rhetoric of the party and the new government suggested a platform of populism, not uncommon in systems of this kind when they have reached social crisis. But populism does not constitute a program or policy, and this the new government eventually found by taking recourse to its historic doctrine, recently however muted, of socialism. Democratic socialism was now given a programmatic content, and asserted as the alternative solution for the country's socio-economic problems. This populist response (though not the specific content of socialism) was not unlike the political response of the government of Trinidad and Tobago after the uprising in that country of 1970. This complement of populism and socialism took the form of acceptance of the policy of non-alignment as the central feature of the government's political foreign policy, and along with that, acceptance of the thesis of national liberation. This thesis suggested that Caribbean regimes themselves should define the parameters of their external relations activities; that the American hemispheric security system and its assumptions should not necessarily take precedence as the determining framework of their international relations. Later the diversification of their external relations with countries to which the United States was not necessarily sympathetic was to be legitimated by the doctrine of "ideological pluralism," originally formulated by Venezuela.

This then, was the kind of domestic socio-political context in which some of the Caribbean regimes undertook the regional normalization of relations with Cuba, and began to explore the possibilities of relations with the socialist bloc — perhaps the most extreme of these explorations being the Guyana application for membership in the Council for Mutual Economic Assistance (COMECON). Those countries, for example Guyana but to some extent Jamaica, which sought particularly close relations with the communist bloc, while pursuing alternative domestic solutions, now sought also to restructure their domestic economic and political institutions in ways more appropriate to the effective conduct of relations with the socialist countries. This was, in part, the rationale for the decisions to move somewhat away from the orthodox Westminster institutional system which they had inherited from the British.

But these various innovations in internal and external policy began to disturb American perceptions of the Caribbean countries' acceptance of the rules relating to hemispheric security; and even more importantly, of the rules relating to foreign investment and the political attitudes and forms that should accompany those rules. The Jamaican refusal of international arbitration after its implementation of its bauxite levy, provided a particularly important instance of the developing American sense of unease. It should be said also that these various innovations began to disturb the local dominant socio-economic sectors, a factor which marked the beginning of a certain coincidence of interest between these local sectors and segments of the American economic and political systems. In Jamaica, by 1975, this unease indicated the end of the government's attempt to conduct policy on the basis of broad national ("all-class") unit. (In Guyana this was already the case much earlier on.)

Thus by the end of the Nixon-Kissinger-Ford regimes, the relationships between some of these countries (Jamaica, Guyana) and the American government and companies had become strained. This strain was characterized by a slowing down of economic assistance, of investment, and by Caribbean claims and American denials of "destabilization." In effect, the national liberation orientation was beginning to come up against the known facts of the small, dependent, character of Caribbean economies, and their vulnerability to external political/economic pressure. The decline of the Jamaican and Guyanese economies by 1976 indicated the problem. The pressures which were now initiated against these governments were intended to reverse the national liberation orientation. (We are not, of course, here saying that external pressures were solely responsible for the decline of the economies.)

The Nixon-Kissinger-Ford approach of subtle, persistent, more often than not covert, pressure, was one response to the changes in Caribbean foreign policy. It was being undertaken at a time when American policy was in general being subordinated to the internal and external effects of Watergate and the failure of the Vietnam adventure; and when, also, the national liberation orientation appeared to have, still, local Caribbean support and popularity. The political crisis concerning the ethics of intervention by the United States was at its height (1975–76). One need only compare the debates in the American congress then (which resulted in the Clark Amendment), with the sense of confidence and legitimacy with which Arthur Schlesinger writes in *A Thousand Days* of the American determination of the nature of the Guyanese regime in 1964, to get a sense of the difference in political climates.

The new Carter administration (Carter-Young-Vance we might say), sought at first to accept the apparent constraints on American international policy, the relatively greater presence in global relations of the Soviet Union, and that country's assertion of the necessity to continue détente and 'normalization' of international relations. In the Caribbean, it appeared to accept the view of the necessity for reorganization of domestic structures and domestic economic policies, so as to make the regimes more capable of coping with socioeconomic crises. The administration accepted the view also (already partially accepted by Kissinger), that a normalization of relations should take place regionally in the Caribbean and Central America, by beginning the process of resolution of Cuban-United States problems, and concluding resolution of the Panama Canal issue.

TWO VIEWS OF CUBA'S RELATIONSHIP

Two differing views about approaches to Cuba, characterized American and Latin American attitudes towards that country: The first was the view indicating the necessity for isolation of Cuba, either (a) to cause maximum domestic difficulties for, and therefore dissatisfaction with, the regime at home; or (b) on a medical analogy of Cuba as a virus, to inhibit the infection of other regional countries. The second view, which began to gain adherents in the late 1960s, was that the first approach had definitively failed, and that the best approach was to attempt to draw Cuba into a network of economic and other arrangements in the region/hemisphere that would induce on her part continuing cooperation with various important countries; and at worst, entail recognizable sanctions for initiating disorder. This process of "opening" to Cuba can be seen in the shift by Argentina in the early 1970s to extensive trade and financial credit relations with her; and in discussions about the possibilities for a triangular Venezuela-Cuba-USSR arrangement on petroleum supplies for Cuba.

It is generally accepted that the Cuban military assistance to the Popular Movement for the Liberation of Angola (MPLA) in Angola, and then to the revolutionary regime in Ethiopia, were the occasion for a new disintegration of the gradually developing bipartisan approach to Cuba in the United States. We should, on the other hand, note that Cuba's assistance to Angola was supported by two Caribbean governments, and tacitly assisted by a third. But these Cuban activities also mark a break in the developing process of harmonizing of approaches to Cuba among Anglophone Caribbean governments; Trinidad taking the view that for small countries, non-intervention on such issues is the appropriate diplomatic approach. A certain diplomatic cohesion within CARICOM as an institution also began to loosen, leading the Trinidad Prime Minister to question in 1979 whether there might any longer be a basis for coordinated diplomacy within the grouping.

The Prime Minister of Trinidad, in making these observations, alluded also to the fact that domestic economic difficulties in major Caribbean states were contributing to the distortion of the attempt to undertake coordinated external activities. This developing diversity of external relations, especially as it related to the world socialist bloc and to the more radical section of the non-aligned movement, began to take on, for the Carter administration also, the aura of hostility to the United States. The administration's response was, in brief, to begin a process of ceasing its policy of differentiation between states on the basis of the efforts that they might be making to reorganize domestic economic structures and policies (for example its support for Jamaica in its relations with the International Monetary Fund (IMF) while not being necessarily sympathetic to the government's foreign policies). Instead the administration now began to place emphasis in its relations with the states, on their attitudes to security and external relations questions.

In practice, this meant not overt acts of hostility to countries like Jamaica and Guyana: not so much acts of commission, as acts of omission. That is, no assistance—private or public—would be given where the US had not been previously obligated to do so, where such assistance might have been useful in allowing the government greater domestic flexibility. Assistance would be given to the governments, or to sectors within the societies, where this coincided with the American national interest. Given the known vulnerability of these countries, deriving from location and economic dependency, such pressures could have multiple effects on the local economies and socio-economic systems. This policy of "hands off" took place—in both Jamaica and Guyana—in the context of their recourse (*de jure* or *de facto*) to IMF stabilization agreements that led inevitably, to major social difficulties, placing governments on the defensive at home, at the same time as their external contexts were becoming increasingly rigid and restrictive.

This conjuncture of internal and external difficulties had one of two effects: either radicalization of external policies to counter or alleviate domestic political (and party) pressures, this radicalization itself then inducing further hostility from the United States; or an increase in internal domestic control and repression, in order to effect the stabilization policies, a recoil from radical external policies deemed hostile to the US, and a certain acceptance of American security definitions.

In this atmosphere, the revolution in Grenada, led by the New Jewel Movement, with its partiality to Cuba, was enough to reinforce and maximize the American concern with security. Economic aid, now more than ever, became the handmaiden of security stabilization; an orientation reinforced by electoral/political changes in St. Lucia and

Dominica, simple-mindedly read, in the climate, as instances of radical change. Then, in the context of the dispute over American policy in respect of Nicaragua in a developing electoral season in the United States itself, came the spectre of the development of tight diplomatic relations between radical governments in a manner not hitherto in existence, across the whole breadth of the "American Mediterranean": Nicaragua-Cuba-Jamaica-Grenada-Guyana. It is an open question whether, for American diplomacy, the development of coherent Caribbean-Central American relations or alliances, unmediated by American interest and power, is acceptable. What, nevertheless, is noticeable is an American orientation towards differentiation of policies towards the areas deemed possibly hostile—Jamaica, Guyana, the Lesser Developed Countries, within the broad context of security stabilization diplomacy.

THE REAGAN DIPLOMACY

It is, in fact, a short step from this general line of the Carter administration (in which the Young-Vance influence had given way to that of Brzezinski) to the Reagan administration policies—harking back to an earlier period and approach, of concentration on security in the region, differentiating between firm allies and others, and isolation of Cuba. In a sense, the groundwork for the reinforced security oriented policies of the new administration, had been prepared in the last phase of the Carter regime.

This is welcome, it should be said, to some governments in the region, operating with an awareness of weakness and dependence exacerbated by the continuous petroleum price explosion and minimum regional cohesiveness. In such an environment, there have tended to develop policies of seeking to derive resources on the basis of proven allegiance to the dominant power.

We can perceive three cross-currents, or potential countervailing forces, to this attempt at reassertion of American dominance. First, there has been a certain reinvigoration of interest on the part of Europe, with its doctrines of social and Christian democracy. This re-invigoration derives not simply from ethicial considerations about the legitimacy of social change and resistance to dictatorship in Latin America. It derives, also, from as the case of European-Middle Eastern relations demonstrate, a perception of self-interest in an international economic climate of increasing "struggle for the world product" in Helmut Schmidt's phrase. It leads to a concern on the part of European countries, that active, unilateral interventionism propelled by domestic forces and interest groups in the United States, may lead to an American distortion of the general socio-economic environment, and hinder their (the Europeans') attempts to construct an environment in which there is a continuity of access to crucial commodity requirements, and availability of markets. Such a concern leads, from time to time, to divergences of interests and policies in the Third World, between Europe and the United States. This is the relevant interpretative framework of the spread of European social/Christian democratic trends, and of the competition within Latin America between them. Attention to the Caribbean represents in part a spill-off from this.

A second countervailing current is the rise of the so-called middle powers in Latin America, and particularly in the Caribbean-Central America area: Venezuela and Mexico. Such countries, as is well perceived by now, have the potential for playing either "proxy" roles, or limited but important "buffer" rules, vis-à-vis American policy. We might simply note here what we can call recent Venezuelan "assertive interventionism," and Mexican "protective diplomacy" in contemporary Caribbean-Central American regional relations. Of course, these countries' still asymmetric relationships with the United States constitute important parameters in the regional role-playing which they can undertake. So too does the fact of structural incoherences in their domestic economic and social systems. But clearly Mexico, for example, now perceives that certain forms of American interventionism in the region not only increase diplomatic instability in the area, but can give rise to internal pressures on her own government—whether from local factions hostile to such interventionism, or from growing numbers of migrant exiles from other countries. Her own domestic political relations could therefore, as a result, become complicated.

Third, there is the perception that there are still not in existence, new and viable economic strategies capable of dealing with the problems that gave rise to the crises in Caribbean states in the first place, even after the boom years of the 1960s. Certain questions arise here. Is more massive capital-intensive investment in the short term likely to make any major impact on the unemployment problem in Jamaica, even if the optimal local climate is provided? Are foreign investors interested in labor-intensive agro-industrial enterprises with longer lead times for recovery of investments than the mineral industries? Is the functioning of the Guyanese economy, in the medium term, dependent perhaps not so much on foreign investment in bauxite or massive hydro-electricity schemes, but rather on the rationalization of local racial-political relations that will allow incentives to those involved in the major agricultural sectors there—a problem not susceptible to external solution? Can regional planning take place in the Eastern Caribbean without major innovation in the local political institutions, so as to permit predictability in the functioning of regional and supra-national institutions? Is the functioning of such cooperation institutions compatible with an emphasis on bilateralism in economic aid between the United States and the Caribbean countries, which while providing political leverage and visibility for the donor, reinforces the tendency to competition between the Caribbean countries themselves?

It is ironic that the current protagonists in the Caribbean, in the private economic and in the political sectors, of the American free enterprise way, do not recognize the historical fact of the major effort at innovation in political institution-making among the separate states in the United States that set the trend at the end of the 18th century for a slow but continuous continental harmonization and centralization of decision-making structures (private and public) there. Nonetheless, there is now a dawning realization in the Caribbean at least, that the problems of the social systems of say, Jamaica and Dominica, have little to do with the presence or absence of Cubans in those territories.

Still, however, the view appears to be prevalent, and emphasized by American emissaries, that it is necessary to reinforce the security systems of these countries, as a prerequisite to their economic development. This harks back, of course, to the philosophy applied in Southeast Asia in the 1960s, the popularized by then Secretary of State Robert McNamara, emphasizing what was taken to be the key linkage between national security and economic development. In Latin America, this took the form of the close relationship between the Alliance for Progress economic programs, and programs of counter-insurgency; the alleged economic successes of the post-1964 Brazilian regime were seen as justifying this approach.

The fact of the matter is, however, that in small countries, the reinforcement of the local security systems leads to an upsetting of the balance between the various socio-political sectors in the countries, giving the military, or national security sector, a decisive weight and a tendency to eventual preeminence in the political systems. This is, and is likely to be the case for two reasons additional to their mere technological dominance. First, with few exceptions, the political party systems, as conciliating and legitimating structures or mechanisms in the Caribbean countries are still weak. Within the context of their lack of capacity for solving mass economic problems, their 'moral' strength weakens, and becomes incapable of counter-balancing the apparent strength of the modernized security forces. Second, the process of modernization of the security forces has a strong ideological content, in addition to its technological content. Already, in the Western tradition, set apart from society, the modernization process suggests to the military a sense of their particular status as the only virtuous sector—as the guardians of the system. Since in small countries the unnatural institutional segregation of the military cannot supersede the traditional social reality of kinship and other such networks, their assumption of political power is likely to be soon tainted by the divisions and social competitiveness of the society. This sets the basis for the coup and counter-coup syndrome.

Thus the emphasis on security is ultimately destructive of the society. It further draws the United States into the local political system, establishing the country and its representatives as the ultimate mediators of the local political system. Such influence can of course even be seen as benign, as in the case of the assurance of the election of Guzmán in the Dominican Republic. But it ultimately de-legitimizes the local government and political elite itself. If then, this model is applied to the newly independent Caribbean, the results can only be similar to those characterizing the older Caribbean, and most of Central America. It is therefore important that the Caribbean leadership, today frequently crippled by the local economic disorder and social pressure, not succumb to this model.

There is no substitute for the endeavour, however faulty and faulting, or regional cooperation and integration of these relatively small national systems, supported by substantial technical and economic assistance by the major metropoles. And though the point is still not accepted by many of the region's academics and political intelligentsia, there is the possibility that the strengthening of the regional system can have an important, though not determining, influence on national social integration. Here again, the geographically peripheral countries, Mexico and Venezuela, will play a role in the determination of the mode of cooperation that can develop; as also in the resolution of the question of whether regional cohesion in the West Indies and Central America will develop within parameters that give primacy to unilaterally adduced US notions of hemispheric interests; or whether, at a minimum, the concerns of national liberation and Third World country economic and political alignments will qualify the influence of those parameters.

BRIEF BIOGRAPHY

NAME	Vaughan Allen Lewis
DATE OF BIRTH	May 17th, 1940
ACADEMIC DEGREES	Ph.D. University of Manchester, 1970
	M.A. University of Manchester, 1963 (Economics)
	B.A. University of Manchester, 1962 (Economics)

VAUGHAN A. LEWIS

ACADEMIC AFFILIATION

Director-General, Organization of Eastern Caribbean States, Central Secretariat, 1982–Present

Director, Institute of Social and Economic Research, University of the West Indies, Jamaica, 1977–1982 (Rank of Full Professor)

BOOKS

M.R. Davies and V.A. Lewis, *Models of Political Systems*, (London: Pall Mall Press, 1971)

Size, Self-Determination and International Relations The Caribbean, (Ed) Institute of Social and Economic Studies (ISER) UWI, Jamaica, 1976

The Political Economy of Independence for the Leeward and Windward Islands, (with A. McIntyre and P. Emmanuel). (Report of the Technical Committee of the Constitutional Advancement for the W.I. Associated States, 1975

ARTICLES

"Integration, Domination and the Small State System: The Caribbean" (with A.W. Singham) in Sybil Lewis and T. Matthews (Eds.) *Caribbean Integration* (University of Puerto Rico, Institute of Caribbean Studies, 1967)

"The Commonwealth Caribbean and Self-Determination in the International System" in Lewis, 1976

"The Idea of a Caribbean Community: LDC's and MDC's and Political Integration," New World Occasional Pamphlets, No. 9, 1974

"The Bahamas in International Politics: Issues Arising for an Archipelago State," *Journal of Inter-American Studies and World Affairs* Vol. 16, No. 2, May 1974

"Political Change and Crises in the English-Speaking Caribbean", in A. Adelman and R. Reading, (Eds.), *Confrontation in the Caribbean Basin* (University of Pittsburgh, Centre for Latin American Studies, 1984).

"Small States and Foreign Policy: The Caricom States from the 70's to the 80's", in J. Heine and L. Manigat, *The Caribbean and World Politics* (Holmes and Meier, 1986)

OTHER INFORMATION

Member of Expert Group on *Caribbean Integration in the 1980's* (Chairman: William Demas).

Consultant to Unitar—Training of Diplomats in the Caribbean LDCs

Consultant to CARICOM/ECLA—Study on the Caribbean Relations with Latin America

Chairman, Task Force on the St. Lucia Morne Education Complex, 1983

Chairman, Board of Governors, Sir Arthur Lewis Community College, St. Lucia

Absorbing the Caribbean Labor Surplus: The Need for an Indigenous Engine of Growth

RANSFORD W. PALMER

Caribbean peoples historically have not had many options. Their ancestors did not opt for leaving Africa; they were taken. And when they arrived in the Caribbean, they did not opt for colonialism; it was the established institution. Even the West Indies Federation which was to have replaced colonialism was not a Caribbean option; it was in fact a metropolitan perception of what the Commonwealth Caribbean ought to have become. Regrettable as it may have been to many, the breaking away of Jamaica in 1961 was probably the first real exercise of a political option by an English-speaking Caribbean people. While national political independence has indeed stimulated Jamaicans and other Caribbean peoples to reach for indigenous resources, their economic options are still by and large controlled by external engines of growth.

Centuries of colonialism and countless analyses of the limitations of small size have indoctrinated the Caribbean into perceiving its economy as defined exclusively by external forces. Consequently, post-independence development strategies were largely predicated upon metropolitan decisions to enlarge the market for Caribbean exports and to increase the supply of capital and technology for their production. But experience has indicated that these external decisions also encouraged a pattern of growth and development that reinforced the priorities of the external decision makers. As a reaction, Caribbean governments during the 1970s began to underscore the need for growth and development patterns that reinforce domestic priorities. For such patterns to become truly operational, the Caribbean must systematically build an indigenous engine of growth capable of exploiting external opportunities.

LOCAL OWNERSHIP

Political independence has provided the vehicle for asserting the economic sovereignty necessary for mobilizing a country's resources in accordance with its national development priorities. For many Caribbean countries, the assertion of economic sovereignty has taken the form of the localization of ownership through nationalization of major industries, as well as through joint-venture arrangements. These strategies are a reaction to the progressive transnationalization of the region during the 1950s and 1960s, a time when Caribbean governments pursued "industrialization by invitation" strategies.

While local ownership is a necessary step in the pursuit of national development priorities, it certainly is not a sufficient one. For even if 100% of everything is locally owned, the Caribbean will not be able to reduce its vulnerability to external shocks without the backward and forward linkages being in place. The task of local ownership therefore is to direct resources into the development of those linkages which the lack of local ownership has ostensibly allowed to lie fallow. Nationalization of the so-called commanding heights of local economies may not by itself enhance the performance of this task, simply because no new investment resources are created by such ownership. One might even argue that there is likely to be a net reduction in resources, since the national acquisition of ownership usually must be paid for out of future tax revenues. Thus the initial benefits from local ownership through nationalization may be limited to national pride.

In the long run, the extent to which the nationalization enhances domestic control over the process of structural transformation will depend on the competitiveness of these industries in international markets and the growth of these markets. If the acquisition of national ownership by itself will not enhance the performance of exports in these markets, neither will it increase the flow of profits for investment in structural transformation. The recent economic history of Jamaica is a clear illustration of this. National ownership of the sugar and bauxite industries and portions of the hotel industry in the 1970s was followed by declining production.

Yet some measure of national ownership is desirable when essential institutions with the power to mobilize resources are dominated by foreign corporations. Financial institutions easily come to mind. It is not surprising that in many developing countries, not only have governments acquired a substantial share of the ownership of private financial institutions, but they have also established complementary public financial institutions to mobilize financial resources as an essential first step toward the creation of greater employment opportunities and the ultimate reduction of the surplus labor.

ANATOMY OF THE LABOR SURPLUS

Because the magnitude of the surplus labor in the English-speaking Caribbean is greatest in Jamaica, it is worth focusing on the data for Jamaica. I have arbitrarily chosen the unemployment data for 1979, the year which, according to the *Economic and Social Survey*, was characterized by "abnormally depressed labor market conditions." But I could just as well have chosen 1978 or 1980 since in all these years, the unemployment rate exceeded 25%.

In October 1979, according to the Department of Statistics, the number of persons unemployed in Jamaica was 299,100 out of a total labor force of 962,500, yielding an unemployment rate of 31%. In developed countries such a national unemployment rate would mean an economic depression of cataclysmic proportions. In developing countries, it is regarded as just one of the characteristics of underdevelopment.

The Jamaican government defines the unemployed labor force as "all persons who were actively seeking work as well as those persons who although they were not actually seeking work indicated that they were willing to accept a job and were in a position to do so." And it classifies the unemployed into "seekers of jobs" and "non-seekers of jobs." Those who were classified as non-seekers answered "None" to the question "What steps did you take to get a job?" Of the 299,100 reported unemployed persons in October 1979, 60% were classified as non-seekers. The main reason put forward for their not seeking jobs is the "relative unavailability of jobs in many areas." It could be argued, however, that many of the non-seekers opted for leisure rather than take jobs which did not fulfill their income and social expectations, and that they were able to make this choice because they could rely on what Henry Bruton calls a "sharing mechanism" that would sustain them until they found a job. This argument is reinforced by the data which show that 53% of the documented unemployed were under the age of 25, and that an almost identical percentage (54%) of those unemployed were supported by parents, guardians, or other relatives, while 28% were supported by spouses or common-law partners. It is of interest to note that twice as many non-seekers (35%) as seekers (17%) were supported by spouses or common-law partners. The main reason for this imbalance is the predominance of females among the non-seekers. The October 1979 data show 139,100 female non-seekers compared to 41,000 male. Of the males, only 800 received spousal and common-law support, while 63,100 of the females did.

Despite the support mechanism that sustains the unemployed, the problem of poverty associated with unemployment and under-employment in the Caribbean is severe. For as Trevor Farrell reminds us in his analysis of unemployment in Trinidad and Tobago, "the argument that unemployment among the young and dependent bears no necessary link with household poverty ignores the fact that there is an operant class system. As such, one suggests that unemployed, dependent youth are likely to come disproportionately out of poor, proletarian households without 'connections' and which need extra income, rather than out of affluent middle-class households. This means that unemployment will in fact tend to correlate with poverty" (*Social and Economic Studies*, June 1978). Moreover, there is the likelihood that a permanent group of unemployables will develop — people who have been out of work for so long that they are unable to acquire the right kind of attitudes that success in a hierarchical work environment requires.

AN INDIGENOUS ENGINE OF GROWTH

How rapidly the Caribbean economy absorbs its surplus over the next two decades depends on its success in generating locally-rooted economic impulses to create employment. Currently, the primary employment-creating impulses reside for the most part in North America and Europe, where the high value-added created by each worker assures a high level of demand for a complex market basket of goods and services. In the current international scheme of things, the Caribbean caters to this demand through the export of raw and semi-finished products whose local value-added is typically low. Through the trickle-down mechanism of international trade, the expansion of demand in North America and Europe increases employment in the Caribbean. In recent years this external engine of growth has begun to slow down.

As long as Caribbean countries remain small open primary-goods-exporting economies, the character of the trickle-down mechanism of international trade will be governed by the pace of growth of the industrial users of these goods, whoever they may be. It is the industrial bias of this trickle-down mechanism that an indigenous engine of growth must exploit. Indigenous engines of growth are industrial sectors which intensively use local raw materials, labor, capital, and managerial expertise to produce for the local as well as for the foreign market. This implies substantial local ownership as well as a low share of imports in the total production cost of finished products.

Like Clive Thomas, I argue that "a effective industrialization strategy must seek the vertical integration of the demand structure with domestic resource use." But unlike Thomas, who espouses production for domestic needs within a context of comprehensive planning and progressive disengagement from international capitalism, I see the aggressive exploitation of international markets as an essential function of an indigenous engine of growth. The fact that a development strategy encourages indigenous development does not mean that it must disengage the economy from the rest of the world. The real test of a strategy of indigenous industrial development is the extent to which it allows a small economy to exploit the markets of the world. Here I draw support from Bela Belassa who argues that: "The flexibility of the national economy is greater under an outward-oriented than an inward-oriented strategy. In the former case, firms have been exposed to competition in world markets and have acquired experience in changing their product composition in response to shifts in foreign demand. By contrast, under inward orientation, there is generally limited competition in the confines of the narrow domestic market and firms have little inducement to innovate, which is necessary under outward orientation in order to meet competition from abroad" (*World Development*, January 1982). The extent to which this indigenous engine will absorb local labor will depend not only on its success in exploiting foreign markets but also on the labor intensity of the production methods adopted.

MANUFACTURING

Whatever comparative advantage Jamaica has had in manufacturing for the export market has been in the production of those goods with a local resource base. The outstanding examples are alcoholic beverages, tobacco, and tobacco products. These were the only manufacturing industries which experienced growth in real output during the declining 1970s. Most of the others operated far below capacity because the drying up of foreign reserves severely restricted the import of raw materials and equipment. Thus as we move from the local resource base end of the manufacturing spectrum to those industries with a predominantly foreign resource base, the performance (and therefore the competitive position) of the manufacturing sector tended to deteriorate. Yet if the manufacturing sector is to develop a strong indigenous core, the growth of such import-dependent industries as petroleum refining and machinery and equipment which provide intermediate inputs for other industries is crucial.

While a domestic raw material base facilitates the development of comparative advantage in a number of manufacturing industries, it is not a sufficient determinant of the indigenous character of an industrial engine of growth. Few would dispute the fact that the large chocolate manufacturing industry in Hershey, Pennsylvania, has been an indigenous engine of growth for that city. Yet America does not produce cocoa beans. Indeed, throughout much of the advanced industrial world, many indigenous engines of growth have been built on raw materials produced in distant developing countries. Perhaps more than most industrial countries, Japan has shown that an indigenous industrial development can be based on imported raw materials. Yet as critical as these raw materials are, they represent a relatively small share of the total cost of industrial production in these countries.

The small size of Caribbean countries has frequently been displayed by economists as a factor limiting similar development. But the limitations of small size are themselves governed by the stock of human capital and the quality of institutional organization, which together can generate policy decisions that can transcend some of these limitations. In the final analysis, the indigenous character of industrial development is determined by these very decisions.

To understand the evolution of manufacturing as an engine of growth in Jamaica, we must look back a few decades. Following the lead of Puerto Rico in the 1950s, many Caribbean countries actively encouraged the development of light manufacturing industries through industrial incentive legislation. For these small countries with rapidly increasing populations, the opportunity to combine capital and labor with very little land to produce goods for a large number of people had an exotic appeal. And when Arthur Lewis published his path-breaking explanation of the economic growth process in developing countries, he provided policymakers in these countries with the theoretical justification for encouraging the development of a modern industrial sector with light manufacturing as its centerpiece. With beautiful centerpiece. With beautiful simplicity, Lewis argued that the industrial sector would expand by mixing capital with an unlimited supply of labor from the rural sector. As the rural labor surplus is absorbed into higher-paying jobs in the industrial sector, agricultural productivity would rise to meet the increase in the demand for food and raw materials. In reality, this beautifully simple relationship failed to develop in the Caribbean. For one thing, the growth of manufacturing in the 1950s and 1960s was led by import-substitution industries which had only the slimmest of ties with the local agricultural sector. For another, industrial incentives provided by the government had the perverse effect of encouraging the substitution of scarce capital for abundant labor. Mahmood Ali Ayub has encapsulated the Jamaican industrialization experience as follows: "The combination of duty-free or low-duty imports of capital goods, the choice of products designated as approved under the incentive laws, the generous depreciation allowances, and quantitative restrictions on final products have encouraged rather capital-intensive investment in an economy where the unemployment rate averages about 25%" (*Made in Jamaica*,

World Bank Staff Occasional Papers, No. 31, 1981). It is not surprising, therefore, that during most of the 1960s, the share of corporate profits in national income grew from 11% in 1963 to 14% in 1969, while compensation to employees hovered about 61%.

Even during the "socialist" 1970s, when capital investment declined sharply, the lending policies of commercial banks continued to subsidize commercial borrowers by offering them loans at interest rates far below the inflation rate. In 1979, for example, the interest rate on commercial loans made by commercial banks in Jamaica was 11% while the rate of inflation was 29%. This in effect meant that borrowers paid a negative real interest rate of 18%. The interest rate subsidy to borrowers of capital was paralleled by an interest penalty on those who acquired savings deposits out of their wage income. The data for 1979 show that commercial banks in Jamaica paid 7% on savings deposits, which meant that at a 29% rate of inflation, holders of these deposits received a negative real interest rate of 22%.

Given the fact that the price of capital has been artificially lowered by both public and private institutional arrangements, is it any wonder that the development of manufacturing in Jamaica has had a capital-intensive bias? Yet, despite its capital intensive bias, Jamaican manufacturing did show some promise of absorbing a substantial amount of labor. During the period 1969 to 1973, for example, a 1% increase in real manufacturing output generally increased manufacturing employment by 0.6%. Even if we regard this as a low employment response, it meant that a 10% growth in real manufacturing output would absorb labor at a rate twice as fast as that of the growth of the labor force. But in the latter part of the 1970s, the promise died from a combination of local and external shocks: local shocks arising from a political philosophy of state supremacy in economic affairs and external shocks arising from sharp increases in import prices reinforced by exchange rate devaluations. Real manufacturing output plunged from J$400 million in 1980, helping to sink the Jamaican economy into eight consecutive years of negative growth.

Out of the ashes of the 1970s, an interesting statistical phenomenon has emerged. When one looks at the period 1976-1979, one finds that while employment in manufacturing establishments having ten or more workers steadily declined, employment in small establishments (those with fewer than ten workers) steadily rose. The conclusion that we are left to draw from this is that had it not been for small establishments, the overall decline in manufacturing employment would have been more severe. It is not possible to say from the statistics the extent to which workers laid off by large establishments started their own manufacturing enterprises or were absorbed by smaller enterprises. Whatever actually happened, the statistics underscore the importance of the role of the small establishment in the manufacturing sector as an employer of labor. All this suggests that if employment is given top priority in the country's development strategy over the next two decades, small manufacturing establishments should be given special incentives to contribute to that employment. Government policy should not lose sight of the fact, however, that what the unemployed worker needs most is not top priority but a job.

THE FUTURE OF MANUFACTURING EMPLOYMENT

By the year 2000, the Jamaican population is expected to be 3 million, with a labor force of roughly 1.4 million—40% larger than that of 1980. If the manufacturing sector is to employ, say, 20% of that labor force, it would have to expand fast enough to absorb 280,000 workers—a little over three-and-one-half times what it now employs. In other words, it would have to increase employment at an annual rate of 6.6% to employ an additional 200,000 workers. Assuming that the degree of labor intensity of manufacturing remains the same as it was in 1980, i.e., 278 workers producing J$1 million of real manufacturing output (at 1974 prices), then total real manufacturing output would almost quadruple by the year 2000 to slightly over J$1 billion, assuming an annual growth rate of 6.6% over the twenty-year period. Thus, given the labor intensity of production, the rate of growth of manufacturing employment would be the same as that of real output. To maintain the same labor intensity, capital investment would have to grow at the same rate as employment.

If we assume, conservatively, that it takes a modest J$5,000 of capital to create a job place, then in order for manufacturing to create 200,000 job places between 1980 and 2000, J$1 billion (at 1980 prices) would have to be invested in that sector alone. Whether or not this kind of investment is forthcoming will depend among other things upon the prospects of quadrupling the market for manufactured output.

Any flow of large amounts of subsidized private foreign capital into manufacturing enterprises will present Jamaica with another dilemma. Large amounts of labor will be absorbed only if wage rates remain low. And only a large permanent stock of surplus labor can ensure this. In other words, we have a paradoxical situation in which the absorption of cheap labor is dependent upon the existence of a permanent pool of surplus labor. This is so because every unit of reduction in surplus labor will increase wage rates which in turn will encourage the substitution of subsidized capital equipment for labor. As wage rates increase, some wage threshold will be reached where additional private foreign investment will absorb only those workers whose marginal productivity equals or exceeds their wage rate. This means that the character of the demand for labor will change from cheap labor to skilled labor. The speed with which this change occurs depends, among other factors, upon the climate of industrial relations. It is not inconceivable that the militancy of labor unions may enter as a factor influencing the choice of production technology by new manufacturing enterprises.

If that critical wage threshold is reached before the stock of cheap, unskilled, surplus labor is significantly reduced, then government policy must direct its attention to transforming the surplus labor into skilled labor. This is easier said than done. Because most of the surplus labor in the Caribbean is young—it is by definition unskilled. Despite their relatively high rate of literacy, their local primary and secondary education does not prepare them for work. They must rely on the workplace itself to do that. If there is no workplace, there is no on-the-job training; if there is no on-the-job training, workers cannot acquire the necessary skills; and if they do not have the skills, certain types of capital investment will not take place.

In a market economy, the creation of workplaces is largely a function of private investment which is itself a function of profits, so that the possibilities for on-the-job training are intertwined with the possibilities for profit. But because the workplace is really an extension of the vocational education system in the Caribbean, its creation should not be dictated by expectations of private profit alone. It should be consciously shaped by public policy and, where necessary, public investment.

The transformation of surplus labor into skilled labor is essential for the functioning of an indigenous engine of growth. But this problem is complicated by the high propensity of Jamaicans to emigrate. The figures show that professional and technical workers as well as those classified as factory operatives emigrated to North America in great numbers during the 1960s and 1970s. All took with them varying amounts of local investment embodied in their education and training. A small country cannot build up an indigenous engine of growth on imported foreign capital if it simultaneously exports its own human capital. Such an exchange is more likely to strengthen the external engine in the long run, since the return flow of profits and interest payments on imported capital is never offset by the remittances received from equivalent human capital exports. The persistence of this adverse balance of payments on human and financial capital flows lays the foundation for a treadmill rather than for an engine.

The fundamental challenge facing Caribbean economies is the absorption of the growing pool of surplus labor into productive activity. Traditionally, domestic employment growth has been largely influenced by foreign demand for Caribbean exports and to a lesser extent by foreign investment in the Caribbean. But over the past decade, the growth of exports and the inflow of foreign capital have slowed considerably. One is left to conclude, therefore, that the extent to which the Caribbean can absorb its surplus labor is limited by its excessive dependence on an external engine. While that will always be important, the need for an indigenous engine that can expand exports when the external engine slows down is urgent. Needless to say, this requires the full support of public policy. Not only must government provide the right kind of environment in which small efficient firms can develop and establish a network of backward and forward linkages with larger firms, it must also actively support innovative export promotion strategies.

One of the most frequently cited obstacles to Caribbean industrial development has been the small size of the Caribbean market. If the US Congress ultimately declares the American market wide open to Caribbean exports, as is proposed in the Caribbean Basin Initiative, then the potential market for Caribbean exports would transcend the traditional limitations of small size. But the removal of market size limitation by legislation unmasks other limitations which are essentially rooted in the underdevelopment of the region. Chief among these is the deficiency in the level and diversity of its human capital stock needed to build and operate the indigenous engine. Only when this engine is on track can the Caribbean fully exploit the opportunities a larger market would provide.

REFERENCES

Ayub, Mahmood Ali (1981) *Made in Jamaica: The Development of the Manufacturing Sector*, World Bank Occasional Papers, No. 31, Baltimore: The John Hopkins Press.

World Bank (1978) *Employment and Development of Small Enterprises* Washington, D.C.: World Bank.

Belassa, Bela (1982) "Structure Adjustment Policies in Developing Economies" *World Development* (January): 28.

Bruton, Henry (1974) "Economic Development and Labor Use: A Review" in E. O. Edwards (ed), New York: The Ford Foundation/Columbia University Press.

Farrell, Trevor M.A. (1978) "The Unemployment Crisis in Trinidad and Tobago: Its Current Dimensions and Some Projections to 1985" *Social and Economic Studies* 17, 2 (June): 120.

Government of Jamaica, (1981) *Economic and Social Survey 1980* Kingston: The Government Printers.

Government of Jamaica (1972) *National Income and Product 1972* Kingston: The Government Printer.

Lewis, W. Arthur (1980) "The Slowing down of the Engine of Growth," *AEA* (Sept): 554–564.

Lewis, W. Arthur (1963) "Economic Development with Unlimited Supplies of Labor" in A.N. Agarwala and S. P. Singh (eds), *The Economics of Underdevelopment* New York: Oxford University Press: 400–449.

Palmer, Ransford W. (1984) *Problems of Development in Beautiful Countries*, Lanham, Maryland: The North-South Publishing Company.

Thomas, C. Y. (1974) *Dependence and Transformation: The Economies of the Transition to Socialism* New York: Monthly Review Press.

BRIEF BIOGRAPHY

NAME	Ransford W. Palmer
DATE OF BIRTH	November 21, 1932
ACADEMIC DEGREES	Ph.D. Clark University, Worcester, Massachusetts, 1966
	M.A. Marquette University, 1962 (Economics)
	B.S. Marquette University, 1961 (Economics)
ACADEMIC AFFILIATIONS	Chairman, Department of Economics, Howard University, 1973-1976
	Associate Dean, Graduate School of Arts and Sciences, Howard University 1974-1976
	Associate Professor, Catholic University of America, 1967-1973
	Central Connecticut State University 1965-1967
	Keuka College 1964-1965

BOOKS

In Search of a Better Life: Perspectives on Migration from the Caribbean, Ed., Praeger, 1990

Problems of Development in Beautiful Countries, North-South Publishing Co., 1984

Caribbean Dependence on the United States Economy, Praeger, 1979

The Jamaican Economy Praeger, 1968

SELECTED ARTICLES

"Education and Emigration from Developing Countries," in *Education and Development*, Lascelles Anderson and Douglas M. Windham, eds. Lexington, Mass.: Lexington Books, 1982.

"Equality, Incentives, and Economic Policy," *American Economic Review*, May 1980, pp. 123-127.

"A Decade of West Indian Migration to the United States, 1961-1972: An Economic Analysis," *Social and Economic Studies*, Vol. 23, No. 4, December 1974, pp. 571-587.

The Caribbean: The Structure of Modern-Conservative Societies

ANTHONY P. MAINGOT

In a geopolitical sense, it is best to define the Caribbean in terms of all the countries that border on that sea. This includes the islands as well as the countries of the mainland whose eastern coasts form the western perimeter of the Caribbean. Together, they form a "basin" of which the sea is the crucial geopolitical feature.

Geographical definitions, however, are ultimately arbitrary things: Their validity depends on the purpose or ends pursued, that is, on their utility. So El Salvador, which has no border on the Caribbean Sea, is regarded by some as a Caribbean Basin country, whereas Mexico, Colombia, and most Central American countries are two-ocean countries yet look more toward the Caribbean than toward the Pacific. A simple explanation lies in the fact that colonization and subsequent trade and cultural contacts developed as part of the Atlantic expansion, first of Spain and later the rest of Europe.

For the purpose of this chapter, "the Caribbean" is considered to be the islands plus those mainland territories that, until recently, were part of the British, Dutch and French colonial empires (see Table 4.1). Clearly, it is difficult to generalize on any level about countries as varied as these. Haiti has almost six times more land and five times the population

TABLE 4.1 Caribbean Territories: Size and Population, 1960 (the poltical pattern reflects the situation in 1967)

	Size		Population		Density of Population
	sq km	%	000s	%	pers./sq km
Independent territories					
Cuba	110,922	47.4	6,743	34.2	61
Dominican Republic	48,734	20.8	3,014	15.3	62
Haiti	27,750	11.9	3,505	17.8	126
Jamaica	11,424	4.9	1,607	8.2	143
Trinidad and Tobago	5,128	2.2	826	4.2	161
Margarita (Venezuelan)	1,150	0.5	76	0.4	66
Barbados	430	0.2	232	1.2	540
Total	205,538	87.9	16,003	81.3	78
Associated with the U.S.					
Puerto Rico	8,897	3.8	2,350	11.9	264
U.S. Virgin Islands	344	0.1	32	0.2	93
Total	9,241	3.9	2,382	12.1	258
French overseas departments					
Guadeloupe	11,729	0.7	275	1.4	159
Martinique	1,080	0.5	267	1.4	247
Total	2,809	1.2	542	2.8	193
Netherlands Antilles					
Windward Islands	68	–	4	–	59
Leeward Islands	921	0.4	192	1.0	209
Total	989	0.4	196	1.0	198
Associated with Great Britain Among the Leeward Islands (St. Kitts-Nevis-Anguilla, Antigua, Barbuda)	843	0.4	111	0.6	132
Among the Windward Islands (Dominica, St. Lucia, St. Vincent, Grenada)	2,127	0.9	320	1.6	151
Total	2,970	1.3	431	2.2	145

TABLE 4.1 Continued

British Colonies					
Cayman Islands	241	0.1	8	–	33
Bahama Islands	11,396	4.9	107	0.5	9
Turks and Caicos Islands	430	0.2	6	–	14
Among the Leward Islands (British Virgin Islands, Montserrat)	258	0.1	19	0.1	74
Total	12,325	5.3	140	0.7	11
Caribbean Islands Total	233,872	100.0	19,694	100.0	84

Source: Helmut Blume,
Note: Totals may not add because of rounding.

of Trinidad and Tobago but only one-fifth the gross domestic product (GDP). Haitians speak Creole, and 80 percent of them are illiterate; Trinidadians speak English, and 95 percent are literate. The former has been governed by dictators throughout its 180 years of independence; the latter had a functioning parliamentary system even before it became independent in 1962.

As with any other geographical region or expression ("Africa," "Latin America," "Asia"), each unit in the region deserves to be studied individually. And yet, there is also value in an understanding of the broader continuities and similarities that make any region a culture area. In the Caribbean, these continuities and similarities result from a blending of modern and conservative features in the composition of major institutions as well as in social and behavioral dynamics. It is useful to call Caribbean societies modern-conservative systems.

THE CONCEPT OF MODERN-CONSERVATIVE SOCIETIES

Like all concepts or heuristic devices in the social sciences, the concept of modern-conservative societies is used to explain complex social structures and social processes. This is especially important in a region as varied as the Caribbean. The point is that the concept appears to describe Caribbean social structure well, and we conclude therefore that it will also help explain the political manifestations of that social structure.

It is important to note that we are not talking about traditional societies: those relatively static, passive, and acquiescent societies generally resistant to change. The modern-conservative society is not only capable of social change, it is often prone to dramatic calls or movements for change. Two cases from the English-speaking Caribbean will illustrate the latent explosive character of the modern-conservative society.

In 1970, the island state of Trinidad and Tobago was suffering both from a decline in oil production and from low prices for oil. OPEC had not yet managed to control the market; it would do this in 1972. The economy had been radically changed by oil. The production of sugar, cacao, and other agricultural commodities was now subsidized; the state became the largest employer. By 1970, there was 22 percent open unemployment and 23 percent hidden unemployment while the unemployment among moderately educated youth (more than eight years of schooling) was 40 percent higher than the average. Additionally, since 80 percent of the percent higher than the average. Additionally, since 80 percent of the women indicated no desire to work, the problem was squarely centered on the young males. These youth were integrated into the modern sector: urban, educated, organized, and in close contact with the outside world. With the Black Power Movement in full bloom in the United States and Canada, two events outside Trinidad lit the spark of Trinidad's own Black Power uprising. One occurred in Jamaica, where authorities prohibited a Guyanese university lecturer, Walter Rodney, from reentering Jamaica from Canada. The so-called Rodney affair stirred the university students in Trinidad as did the "riot" of a dozen Trinidadian students in Canada claiming racial discrimination. Racial grievances, unemployment, unrest among the professional military men, and accusations of graft and corruption against certain government ministers all came to a head in a massive movement against "the system." And yet, the motor, the driving force, was not class conflict but a deep sense of righteous indignation. The target of the movement, Prime Minister Eric Williams, was repeatedly invited to join the moral crusade for black identity and ownership. Clearly, he had lost his moral authority, but not his political legitimacy.

In 1970 in Trinidad, righteous indignation took on psychological and cultural dimensions: a return to history, to a purer and more integral past as a means of collective and individual cleansing and redemption. African names and apparel were adopted and modern European ways rejected to such an extent that the movement's leadership soon began to alienate large sectors of the Indian and colored populations as well as the black middle class. A reorganized police force put an end to the movement; ten years later, the same leaders competed in a free election and were soundly defeated. Had the problems of the society been solved by the massive influx of oil revenues since 1973? Not at all. Fully 83 percent of those who in 1981 felt that life was getting worse on the island attributed that deterioration to corruption.

Although the incumbent party won a sizable electoral victory in 1981, race again showed its strength: The victorious People's National Movement (PNM) won the safe "black" seats; the opposition United Labour Force (ULF), the safe "Indian" seats. As in 1970, a deterioration in the economy could again spark unrest, but it will have to play on certain moral cords and generate a sense of indignation among both leaders and followers, with totally unpredictable outcomes. The case of St. Lucia in early 1982 illustrates this aspect of political behavior in modern-conservative societies.

On January 16, 1982, the prime minister of St. Lucia resigned under pressure. This forced the dismissal of Parliament and mandated the calling of elections within a few months. The caretaker government was led by a member of a radical party, the smallest of St. Lucia's three main parties. It was not this party, however, that had led the antigovernment movement, nor were the issues in the movement ideological ones in the political sense. That movement was headed by the chamber of commerce and other middle sectors, protesting what they regarded as official corruption and abuse of government authority.

The upheaval in St. Lucia was very similar to that which had occurred in Grenada three years earlier: Incompetence, corruption, and abuse of authority had engendered a massive sense of indignation among a multiplicity of sectors. In Grenada, the opposition movement was called the Committee of 21, indicating the number of groups involved in the opposition to Prime Minister Eric Gairy. The difference between Grenada in 1979 and St. Lucia in 1982 was that a small clique managed to wrest power by force of arms in the former, teaching a lesson to the middle classes in the latter. Although all groups participated in the 1982 elections in St. Lucia, the moderates won every seat in the House of Assembly. Similar defeats of radical parties had already occurred in Dominica, St. Vincent, St. Kitts, Jamaica, Barbados, and Trinidad. Elections in the Dominican Republic in mid-1982 also indicated a tendency toward the center in political-ideological terms; it appears to be a Caribbean-wide phenomenon.

These illustrations allow us to identify some of the characteristics of the modern-conservative society. It should at the outset be understood that to speak of "structures" does not imply anything static: It merely means that certain underlying factors or interrelationships are more durable, more tenacious and retentive, than many of the immediate and observable manifestations of those relationships suggest. Such ideas or concepts as history, life, being, and essence are central to this conservative view of life and are logical products of ex-colonial, multiethnic, and deeply religious societies, as we shall see. As Karl Mannheim (1953:77–164) has noted, these patterns of thought, far from becoming superfluous through modernization, tend to survive and adapt themselves to each new stage of social development. Because it has a real social basis, conservative thought is functional and useful as a guide to action.

The modern conservative society, then, tends to mobilize politically around issues that strike chords of a conservative type, issues that engender a collective sense of moral indignation. Mobilization occurs, however, through modern mechanisms and institutional arrangements. The most conservative of values, if widely shared and if the spokesmen have access to modern institutions and mechanisms, can have impacts that have revolutionary manifestations though something less than revolutionary goals—if "revolutionary" implies a complete overthrow of the existing sociopolitical structure, not merely the regime.

The myth of the modern, revolutionary nature of Caribbean societies stems from a misunderstanding of the nature of many of the movements that brought revolutionary elites to power. Even in modern-conservative societies (as Lenin theorized and demonstrated), a determined elite can bring about a designed outcome. This is so because after the initial mobilization, the movement tends to enter into a qualitatively new phase. This phase has dynamics of its own, dynamics that tend to represent a combination of the unpredictability and complexity of all mass actions and the more predictable—or at least understandable—actions of revolutionary cadres and elites. The latter can turn the movement in a revolutionary direction even in modern-conservative societies; they are less capable, however, of initially generating a revolutionary mobilization in such societies.

This explains why the Surinam Revolution (1980) and the Grenadian Revolution (1979), like the Nicaraguan Revolution, had to coexist with strong private sectors, established churches, and other aroused but hardly revolutionary sectors. These regimes were confronted with the complexity of the modern-conservative society. (They were also confronted, of course, by the hostility of the U.S. government, which in 1983 took advantage of internal strife in Grenada to invade and to dismantle the revolutionary government.)

Understanding the nature of political change in these societies, then, requires an analysis not only of the immediate political happenings in the area—the political landscape—but also of what might be called the structural or enduring aspects of Caribbean political dynamics: the political substructure. What is required, thus, is a political economy approach to the area in which demographics and economics are central, though not exclusive, topics of analysis.

CARIBBEAN POLITICAL ECONOMY

In part because it involves modern societies with relatively skilled labor and a high degree of unionization, and thus high wages, the development process in the Caribbean has

TABLE 4.2 Agricultural Employment and Output, Selected Territories, 1960 and 1970 (percentage of total)

	1960		1970	
	Employment	Output	Employment	Output
Barbados	26	28	16	14
Guyana	37	26	29	19
Jamaica	39	12	29	8
Trinidad and Tobago	21	12	16	5
Eastern Caribbean Common Market	46	36	32	22

Source: World Bank, *The Commonwealth Caribbean* (Baltimore: John Hopkins University Press, 1978), p. 119.

tended to be industrial and capital intensive. The overflow of available labor (because of reduced migration) has tended to be absorbed by the public sector. The financial and economic retrenchments made necessary by the energy crisis (and consequent balance-of-payment difficulties) have forced a slowing down of this public employment. The result is not merely unemployment but, rather, a process that is creating a whole generation of "never employed." The vast majority of this group has attained at least some high school education and has aspirations and some skills. Alas, they tend not to be the skills that are in demand nor the aspirations that would encourage needed activities such as agricultural enterprises. Only the latter, with its labor intensity, could in fact absorb the large numbers of people who annually enter the labor market.

Such an agricultural orientation and direction is to be found nowhere in the Caribbean except Haiti, which is still 80 percent rural. The World Bank figures in Table 4.2 give a clear picture of this fundamental fact of Caribbean political economy: the declining agricultural sector. The movement is toward the urban areas and, critically, migration abroad. In the English-speaking Caribbean, migration accounted for a 46,000-person decrease in the labor force during the 1960s. Because of a slowdown in migration, this labor force is calculated to have increased by about 400,000 during the 1970s, two-thirds of the increase being among young adults. On every one of the Caribbean islands, youthful adults make up an ever-increasing percentage of the total population, and everywhere they share the restlessness of youth the world over. But the "complexity" approach cautions that it would be a terrible mistake to associate, a priori, all this modern political ferment and activity with a state of social revolution. Such an association might preempt a closer look at the substratum—the political economy—of Caribbean society. Although the configurations and expressions of this conservatism vary, the following aspects of Caribbean society show great similarities from one country to another.

Throughout the area there is a deep and dynamic religiosity, even though the intensity and pervasiveness of religion—as doctrine and as institutions—do vary. One situation is that of the dominant church in the central plaza being attended by women and children once a week; such was the case in Cuba before the revolution and is the case in Puerto Rico today.[1]

Another situation is that of the English-speaking West Indies, where one finds multiple denominations and many churches scattered throughout neighborhoods, urban and rural. This case illustrates a living presence of religion rather than a ceremonial one and is typical also of countries such as Haiti, where Christianity combined with West African religions to create a syncretism called Voodoo (also called *santería* in Cuba and Shango in Trinidad). This religiosity impinges on other spheres of life.

One attitudinal spin-off from the doctrines of the major religions in the area is the belief in private property, especially land. There is an intense love and respect for the land

and a desire to own a piece of it. The popular Haitian saying *se vagabon qui loue kay* ("only vagabonds rent their homes") expresses the desire for ownership, for full possession. On Nevis, 80 percent of the home owners own their house lot; on St. Vincent, the figure is 75 percent. Although the figure is only 46.8 percent on Barbados, when one travels around that island it is clear that even the smallest house has a name; the name represents the emotional dimension of property ownership. The little picket fence around the house is the physical expression of the emotional dimension. That picket fence (or cactus fence in the Netherlands Antilles) also expresses another characteristic of Caribbean peoples. In the midst of their gregariousness, they like their privacy, an expression of their intrinsic independence. This characteristic, usually identified as a rural phenomenon, is pervasive even in urban areas. This explains the living presence in West Indian language of old English sayings such as "a man's home is his castle" or, as used with an additional meaning in Creole; "two man rat can't live in same hole."

This latter saying expresses the idea that in any house, only one of the partners can wear the pants. It is taken for granted that the male partner does. And yet, these societies are fundamentally matriarchal and matrilocal: Because of the very high illegitimacy rate among the working class, it is the mother who raises the child, and the child lives where the mother (as well as the maternal grandmother) lives. A 1981 study by Gary and Rosemary Brana-Shute demonstrates that there is a deep underlying conservatism in the socialization processes and aspirations of even the hard-core—and angry—unemployed youth in the area.

And yet, as Caribbean history has repeatedly shown, these generally moderate and family-oriented societies, and especially the youth, are capable of sudden, quite unpredictable political and social outbursts. This was very evident in Curacao, in the Netherlands Antilles, in 1969 when a minor industrial strike exploded into a class and race attack on the system. Half of the buildings in the main commercial sector of the island were burned to the ground.

The basically conservative substrata of Caribbean societies also sustain very modern and highly mobilized societies and their corresponding agencies. Note, for instance, the following dimensions and configurations of that modernity: With certain exceptions, such as Haiti, the populations are literate and schooled. On island after island, from 90 to 100 percent of the children of primary school age are in school, and literacy rates everywhere are above 85 percent. Although there is some evidence that conservative attitudes are positively correlated with greater degrees of education (Ryan, Greene, Hanewood, 1979; Maingot, 1979) the fact is that a population that participates in the articulation of grievances and wishes and that can utilize the modern techniques of communication is one that has an increased capability for mobilization. Throughout the Caribbean, people are politically mobilized. There are everywhere political parties and interest groups with capacities for extensive articulation of interests and aggregation of these into policy demands. No government today, of the left, middle, or right, can ignore the demands of the groups. Literacy and education also make the labor union system more effective. In the West Indies, from 30 to 50 percent of the work force is unionized, and historic ties with political parties give unions additional leverage in the bargaining processes.

Another of the modern agencies that a literate and schooled population makes possible is the state bureaucracy, which, according to Max Weber, is the most "rational" of all forms of organization. Such state bureaucracies are found throughout the Caribbean in the form of a relatively skilled public or civil service. In Trinidad, there are three and a half times more people with diplomas or degrees in public service than in the private sector, and in Jamaica, the institutionalization and legitimacy and the public service is evident in its capacity to survive dramatic shifts in political party fortunes. The top echelons of these bureaucracies are now being educated in the area. The University of the West Indies (UWI), with campuses in Jamaica, Trinidad, and Barbados, now makes university education accessible to a much broader sector, as do the universities in Guyana, Martinique, Surinam, Curaçao, and elsewhere. Whereas in 1957 there were 2,632 West Indians studying at universities abroad compared to only 566 at UWI, by 1982 the number abroad had doubled, but the number of students at UWI had increased twelvefold.

Caribbean modernity is reflected also in other areas. The fact that Caribbean working people have largely developed both the habits and the skills required of labor in modern societies has made them very desirable as immigrant workers. This explains the long tradition of migration, and return, of Caribbean workers; they are and always have been a mobile population. Whether building the Panama Canal and Central America's railroads and ports or running the London public transportation system, Caribbean workers have had the attitudes and skills of urban workers. They return with new skills, but also with the hope of buying that house or piece of land for which they have saved. In Haiti, the "Bahamas" house was built with remittances from Haitians working in the Bahamas.

While abroad, Caribbean workers are able to communicate with their countrymen. Note, for instance, the mailboxes along every road, the widespread use of radio and newspapers, direct-dialing telephones from the United States to many islands, and in the French West Indies, Netherlands Antilles, Jamaica, Trinidad, and Barbados, the widespread use of television. Modern communications assist both in modernizing the Caribbean and in preserving ethnic attachments. Literacy in one or more of the major languages of the world (English, Spanish, and French) gives Caribbeans access to the major currents of ideas and technology, while their native variations on those languages (Creole in Haiti, papiamento in Curaçao, taki-taki in Surinam) strengthen the sense of *volk*, or nation, of *gemeinschaft*, or community.

If one adds the fact that any particular sector of the islands is within, at most, a two-hour bus ride of some urban center, one understands something of the modernity of the society as well as its continued proximity to rural village life. Ties to the land and to tradition are not broken by a move to the city; rather, those links provide something of the underpinnings of the conservative values and orientations of the urban residents even as the diversification of memberships and involvements (churches, sport clubs, unions, political parties, service clubs) contribute to and express the society's modern dimensions. The glue that holds all together is the Caribbean family, both the nuclear and the extended family with its *compadres* ("godfathers"), *comadres* ("godmothers"), "cousins," and "aunties."

These, then, are some of the native aspects of these modern-conservative societies. Yet, an analysis of the substrata also has to take into account the external factors affecting change. Although, on balance, internal factors tend to carry more weight in any causal analysis of social change, the small size of the Caribbean states makes external factors somewhat more important than they would be for most states.

There can be no question that smallness makes them vulnerable to a host of problems. One of these is national insecurity, as was illustrated by the extraordinary 1981 attempted invasion and subversion of the Dominica government by U.S. mercenaries in league with local politicians. Furthermore, securing a degree of national representation abroad is costly. But such representation is important not only to facilitate contact with foreign nations through traditional diplomatic ties but also to attract attention from the ever-increasing number of international and multilateral banking or lending agencies.[2]

Also contributing to the vulnerability are the cleavages created by the race and ethnic divisions that characterize the politics of nations such as Trinidad and Tobago, Guyana, and Surinam. In each of these countries, Indians (originally from British India) comprise half or more of the population. Predominantly Hindu in religion (some 20 percent are Muslim), these sectors are in themselves prototypical modern-conservative groups. Reconciling Hinduism with secular ideologies such as Marxism is a difficult task in itself; to do so in a context in which major elements of that Indian population are capitalists, landowners, and merchants (as in the case of Guyana and Surinam) is an even more complex proposition. Whether the cleavage is black vs. white, Indian vs. black, or black vs. mulatto, race and race conflict contribute to social division and to the vulnerability of Caribbean societies. Table 4.3 gives us, in broad strokes, a racial breakdown of those societies.

Understanding and awareness of the vulnerabilities resulting from smallness have led to many attempts at regional or subregional integration. Dreams of a united Caribbean are not new. They were expressed in José Martí's theme that Cuba and Puerto Rico were wings of the same dove; in Haitian President Jean Pierre Boyer's dream of liberating all the slaves, first of neighboring Santo Domingo (which his armies occupied from 1822 to 1844), then of other islands; and in the West Indies Federation, which lasted from 1958 to 1961. The repeated failures of such attempts, however, created skepticism about the viability and, indeed, the desirability of such union.

The mini- and microstate are now a reality of the Caribbean scene. Today, the area limits itself to attempts at economic integration through such instruments as the Carib-

TABLE 4.3 Racial Structure of the Population of the Caribbean Islands, 1960[a]

	Caribbean Islands (total)		Greater Antilles		Lesser Antilles		Bahamas	
	000s	%	000s	%	000s	%	000s	%
Whites	7,800	39.6	7,700	44.6	80	3.4	23	20
Negroes	7,800	39.6	6,000	34.8	1,720	73.2	90	80
Mulattoes	3,670	18.6	3,550	20.6	120	5.1	–	–
Asian Indians	350	1.8	–	–	350	14.9	–	–
Indians and Mestizos	80	0.4	–	–	80	3.4	–	–
Total	19,700	100.0	17,250	100.0	2,350	100.0	113	100

Source: Helmut Blume, *The Caribbean Islands* (London: Longman, 1974).
[a] Approximate figures

bean community (CARICOM) and the Caribbean Development Bank. Even the organization of Eastern Caribbean States (OECS)[3] emphasizes the economic aspects of association, leaving politics, including foreign policy, to each individual member.

Unfortunately, while insularity gathers strength on each island, international politics and transnational forces (including multinational corporations) press for a reduction in state sovereignty. And today, as in the past, size and isolation make these territories targets for international expansion. In the late twentieth century, escalating ideological competition among international forces has made the Caribbean a cockpit, the modern-day equivalent of the European battlegrounds of the seventeenth and eighteenth centuries. Today, the Marxist-Leninist Movement, the Socialist International, the Christian Democrats, and international labor organizations as well as new regional actors such as Cuba, Venezuela, and Mexico have all joined the battle for the minds of Caribbean peoples. the United States has long been engaged in the competition. To these may be added many proselytizing religious and semireligious groups, from Islam to the Seventh Day Adventists to the Rastafarian Movement (now of Pan-Caribbean character). Since the foreign offices and intelligence services of the major states never left the area, the present ideational and ideological scene in the Caribbean is a bewildering panorama of competing radio broadcasts; roaming sports, cultural, and scientific missions; state visits; and sojourning consultants from international aid agencies— and these activities are only the overt ones. While insularity strengthens the barriers to movements of labor, governments pursuing development put out red carpets to entice foreign capital as it moves from one nation to the other.

The structural elements revealed in this bare-boned sketch of external factors tend to contribute to the generalized idea that these societies are potentially revolutionary. To be sure—as the many cases of dramatic political change illustrate—Caribbean societies are not static; they have the capacity and propensity to react with apparent abruptness and even violence against targets of popular grievances and resentments. This capacity is one structural characteristic of political participation in the area. The central questions, however, remain. Who reacts, why, and over what? What do the answers tell us about the ongoing, and therefore relatively predictable, aspects of Caribbean political culture and dynamics? Crucially, what has been the nature of leadership in the area?

POLITICAL-IDEOLOGICAL LEADERSHIP

The career of Trinidad's Prime Minister Eric Williams, who governed from 1956 until his death in 1981, illustrates the complexity of style and orientation of the region's leadership. Much has changed in the Caribbean since 1956, when Williams first came to power as a celebrated scholar-administrator. His Ph.D. thesis at Oxford, "Capitalism and Slavery," had become the standard radical interpretation of European industrialization (made possible by the triangular slave trade) and emancipation (made necessary by the very success of that industrialization). He was living proof that a colored man was indeed capable of great achievements in a mother country's highest centers of learning.

This success and his later "telling off" of the English, Americans, French, and Dutch in the Caribbean Commission—an agency set up by the colonial powers to assist in Caribbean development—were proof sufficient to make him the man to lead the island's decolonization movement. "Massa day done" became William's battle cry, a welcome prospect to the black and colored middle and working classes who followed his charismatic leadership. The psychic scars of colonialism had found their soothing balm. But where to turn for models?

Asia and Africa were also going through the pains and pleasures of decolonization, and those continents—more than neighboring Latin America—provided some, but not all, of the models. It was in the paths of Nehru, Nkrumah, Sukarno, and Kenyatta that Dr. Williams saw represented the post-World War II, nonwhite decolonization process. Like those leaders, Williams understood very early that decolonization had both racial and political connotations. The very concept of empire had been based on ideas of racial superiority and inferiority. These men had to give living rebuttals to the imperial myths that colored peoples could not govern themselves and that non-Western societies could never be viable nations. Not only did they have to prove their people's capacity by leading the political struggle, they also had to prove their personal worth through exceptional achievement. In colonial situations, the burden of proof is always with the colonized.

It is no surprise therefore that more often than not, these decolonizers began to perceive themselves as the very—if not the sole—embodiment of their countries. This perhaps was the genesis of their eventual sense of indispensability. Williams acted for twenty-five years on the belief. Repeated victories at the polls did little to dispel the illusion.

But Trinidad, like the rest of the English-speaking West Indies, was in the Western Hemisphere where the majority of the independent countries were Spanish speaking, and most were far from being democratic models. Surrounded by dictators who enjoyed warm relations with Washington and London, Williams understood that the decolonization of the English-speaking Caribbean was to be a lonely process in the Latin American setting. The parliamentary system adopted by the West Indies differed from the executive system of Latin America, and Williams always felt that the former suited the West Indies better.

This belief was shared by an array of truly exceptional West Indian leaders: Alexander Bustamante and Norman Manley in Jamaica, Grantley Adams and Errol Barrow in Barbados, and Cheddi Jagan in Guyana (a true constitutionalist despite his Marxist rhetoric). By the mid-1960s, these leaders had laid the foundations of West Indian constitutional democracy, thereby giving the lie to colonial racists and modern ideologists who argued that only authoritarian one-party states fit the Caribbean reality.

Williams governed long enough to deal with two elected Manleys, father and son, two elected Adamses, father and son, to see the OPEC-created explosion in revenues from gas and oil, to see the collapse of the West Indian Federation and the rise of the Caribbean Common Market, and to see the decline of Britain and the rise of Cuba and Venezuela as regional powers. He lived long enough to see the rise and fall of Michael Manley's "democratic socialism" in Jamaica (1972–1980), and he appeared ready to deal with Jamaica's new leader, Edward Seaga, who emphasized the role of the private sector.

By the time of Williams's death in 1981, the Caribbean had witnessed many a social and economic experiment and was quite a different area. Although there were some governments "for life" (Cuba, Haiti, and probably also Guyana) there were now democratic governments in virtually all the other Caribbean island states, making the Caribbean the largest area governed by democratically elected regimes in the hemisphere. The parliamentary system was working in the West Indies.

The first generation of postindependence leaders in the English-speaking Caribbean had sown well and, in so doing, left their marks on the immediate postcolonial era. In the 1980s, there was some indication that the passing of that era meant not only generational change but also the passing of the charismatic, "indispensable" man as a part of the political culture. This change is demonstrated by a recent trend in the region's politics: the emergence in the 1980s of the less-than-charismatic "manager" political type. Edward Seaga of Jamaica, Mary Eugenia Charles of Dominica, Tom Adams of Barbados, George Chambers in Trinidad, and Antonio Guzman and Jorge Blanco in the Dominican Republic, all fit this mold.

What explains this shift in leadership? Certainly there is some truth to the view that the trend is partly reactive: a response to the dismal administrative performance of some of the area's most celebrated charismatic leaders of the 1960s and 1970s, Fidel Castro of Cuba, Michael Manley of Jamaica, and Forbes Burnham of Guyana, for example. But a fuller explanation would bring us closer to the issue of complexity that was posited earlier, that dual process involving enduring, underlying relationships, values, and interests (substrata) and the changing political landscape. The careers of Caribbean leaders of Marxist or non-Marxist socialist persuasion, that is, the secular modernizers, are illustrative.

One such case is Aimé Césaire, mayor of Fort-de-France, Martinique, and Communist *député* to the National Assembly in Paris for over thirty-five years. When Césaire resigned from the French Communist Party in 1956, it was a sensational event. "Thinking of Martinique," he wrote, "I see that communism has managed to encyst us, isolate us in the Caribbean Basin." To Césaire, there was an alternative path: "Black Africa, the dam of our civilization and source of our culture." Only through race, culture, and the richness of ethnic particulars, he continued, could Caribbean people avoid the alienation wrought by what he called the "fleshless universalism" of European communism. (1956:15)

This return to history, to culture, and ultimately, to race has been a fairly consistent response to many Caribbean socialist modernizers—who never stop referring to themselves as Socialists—who are faced with the difficulties of attempting secular revolutionary change in largely nonrevolutionary and conservative societies. The counterpoint between a rational and secular universalism and a particularism of "being" has resulted in some original and dynamic West Indian ideological modifications to Marxism and non-Marxist socialist thought. In Césaire's case, it led to his fundamental contributions to negritude, a literary-political movement highlighting African contributions to contemporary society, as well as to an accommodation with continued French-Caribbean integration (though not assimilation) into the French system.

Trinidad's first major socialist activist in the 1920s, Andrew Cirpriani, yearly paid his homages to Fabian thought and the British Labour Party, but after decades of militancy, he withdrew in the face of two challenges to his basic conservative view of the world: the divorce bill, which he saw as a threat to the family, and the use of violence in strike action. Those who used violence (such as Uriah Butler, the leader in Trinidad's 1937 labor movement and uprising) themselves ended up turning to religion (quoting biblical passages) and to history (studying the rule of Henry VIII). The "pull" on the leadership of the conservative values and norms of the masses has been powerful. Even Eric Williams, whose early historical writings were gems of Marxist thought and careful documentation, would eventually abandon what one admirer called "the infinite, barren track of documents, dates and texts" to write "gossip . . . which experience had established as the truth."

A review of Trinidadian C.L.R. James's five decades of thought on socialism and revolution indicates that he never resolved the universalism-particularism counterpoint. In his *The Black Jacobins* (1938),[4] perhaps the most influential West Indian work of the twentieth century, James vacillates and hedges but ends up on the side of the Dessalinean Black Revolution as distinct from the universalist experiment of Toussaint.

It is not at all evident that there can be in practice a working and productive relationship between racial or ethnic populism and a program based on premises of secular modernism, whether socialist or not. Even in theory, the reconciliation appears improbable. A case in point is the work of the Martinican, Frantz Fanon. Like Césaire—whom he knew and greatly admired—Fanon wished to be liberated from the "fleshless shackles" of European thought; thus he searched for a key to what he called the "psycho-affective equilibrium" of the angry Third World intellectual. This search is central to an understanding of the dynamics of modern-conservative societies. Fanon felt compelled to describe and explain what he perceived as the relentless determination of revolutionary elites to return to history: to "renew contact once more with the oldest and most pre-colonial springs of life of their people." Fanon understood the enduring consequences of the racial hurts and angst inflicted during colonialism. "This state belief in national culture," he wrote, "is in fact an ardent despairing turning toward anything that will afford him anchorage." (1968: 217) Even such a lifelong and dedicated Marxist as Guyana's Cheddi Jagan finds a practical, and perhaps even psychological, need to blend his Marxism with an ongoing devotion to Hinduism. Clearly then, race and a desire for a return to history have been powerful forces blocking a universalist and secular approach to politics.

The rational and secular view of the world that is necessary for modern (especially socialist) revolution is not easily sustained in these societies. In the cases of Césaire, Williams, Norman Manley, Forbes Burnham, and others, Marxist or socialist thought was mediated by pressures from the multiethnic, religious, and conservative societies they led—and which eventually forced them to succumb to the particularistic note in the particularism-universalism counterpoint. It is a fundamental characteristic of a conservative society that views of the world and of social change resist any notions of dealing with problems in any way other than in terms of their historically perceived uniqueness. This characteristic has been, more often than not, part of the Caribbean experience.[5]

This experience explains how a Dr. François Duvalier ("Papa Doc") could come into power in Haiti in 1957 advocating a radical Black Power revolution but revert to a very traditional form of political barbarism. He played the most retrograde chords of a deeply conservative society to entrench himself—and then his son, Jean Claude "Baby Doc"—in power.

CONCLUSION

In 1956, the only independent countries in the Caribbean were Cuba, the Dominican Republic, and Haiti. On the mainland, Venezuela was ruled by a dictator, Pérez Jiménez, and Colombia was ruled by another dictator, Rojas Pinilla. By the end of the 1950s, many such dictators were dead or out of office, and a new movement had gained power in Cuba, with Fidel Castro at its head. Although initially espousing the electoral path and a reformist economic program, the Cuban Revolution speedily moved toward a centralized, single-party model accompanied by a rapid socialization of virtually all productive sectors. This was a new model for the Caribbean, though it contained elements that had long been part of the Caribbean political milieu: fear of U.S. intentions, intense nationalism, and a desire to mobilize all the people in a heroic movement of national reconstruction and liberation. The anticolonial movements of the area had a potentially powerful model in Cuba.

The example of the Cuban Revolution, however, has not proved to be as attractive as originally thought. Certainly part of the explanation lies in the perception that the Revolution has been something less than an economic success. But there is also the fact that language, cultural orientation, and the political realities of decolonization have tended to keep the attention of Caribbean societies focused elsewhere. In the English-speaking Caribbean, attempts to create a federation of island states—the West Indies Federation—lasted three years (1958–1961). Subsequently, in the early 1960s, Jamaica, Trinidad and Tobago, and Barbados each moved toward independent status within the British Commonwealth. British Guiana had refused to join the federation but also was moving toward independence by the mid-1960s. The Netherlands Antilles were content to decolonize by expanding the autonomy of their political and administrative systems within the Kingdom of the Netherlands. The French West Indies and Cayenne (French Guiana), made integral parts of France as overseas departments in 1946, appear satisfied with that status. They participate in every aspect of the French social welfare system, but at the same time, each retains its cultural identity and autochthonous political culture.

Within the past two decades, the majority of countries in the area have moved rapidly to consolidate their own political systems. In all the ex-European possessions (with the exceptions in the early 1980s of Grenada and Surinam), political parties and groups operate freely, and human rights appear protected by a range of independent government and private institutions and organizations.

By the end of the 1960s, then, the Caribbean was subjected to various pressures and exposed to several models or sources of attraction and interest:

1. The continued and increasing presence of the United States, which moved to replace the European powers as the major economic partner and strong cultural influence.
2. The Cuban Revolution, which epitomized heroic, popular mobilization.
3. The Puerto Rican model, which appeared to have brought economic development with political freedom.
4. Africa, where a decolonization process had produced charismatic leaders such as Kwame Nkrumah, Jomo Kenyatta, and Julius Nyerere.

Clearly, these models were not always in harmony either in theory or in practice. The attraction of Africa resulted from a heavy dose of racial identification as well as personal associations between leaders who had shared the anti-European sentiments and ideas of preindependence days. This did not harmonize with the appeal of Cuba, which responded to a Spanish American variant of anti-Americanism. The Puerto Rican attraction was a pragmatic one based on what was regarded as a realistic assessment of the region's political economy. Above and among all these attractions was a strong love-hate relationship with the United States. In a region with a predominantly black population, how does one admire the United States with its Jim Crow laws, and yet how does one ignore not only its power but also its sincere, albeit grudging, struggle for civil rights for all?

The "U.S. dilemma" has its own Caribbean counterpart. The desire of Caribbeans for modernity draws their attention to the United States, yet their yearning for liberation and economic justice for themselves (and their African brothers) turns their eyes occasionally toward Cuba. Both sentiments have as context societies with deep attachments to organized religions, private property, and highly diversified and plural social structures. The result is ambivalence and unpredictability. And yet, in many ways, the ebb and flow of Caribbean politics and social change can be illustrated through the metaphor of the counterpoint between the desire and capacity for modernization and change and the strength of conservatism. Each tendency has well-developed idea systems, as well as institutional and organizational representation. Not surprisingly, both tendencies can be found in the vast majority of Caribbean peoples. Thus, it is useful to characterize Caribbean societies as modern-conservative societies, an ideal-type construct that helps us understand what otherwise might appear to be contradictory, or even unintelligible, in the behavior of this multilingual, multiracial, and multistate area.

NOTES

1. Cuba and Puerto Rico were perhaps the least structurally conservative for the Caribbean societies, in large measure, because of the considerable influence of secular North American values and interests.
2. This is not only a question of the asymmetry of power but also a question of commanding respect and dignity.
3. Antigua and Barbuda, St. Vincent and the Grenadines, Dominica, St. Lucia, Grenada, St. Kitts-Nevis, Montserrat.
4. James' book was first published in 1938. A popular edition is the 1963 revised version by Vintage Books.
5. One interesting exception is the New Jewel Movement, which came to power in Grenada in 1979 and which has attempted to portray that experience as an extension of a Caribbean decolonization process begun in Cuba. By 1983, the experiment was snuffed out by internal implosion and the subsequent invasion by the USA.

REFERENCES

Blume, Helmut (1974) *The Caribbean Islands*, London: Logmans.
Cesaire, Aime (1956) "Lettre a Maurice Thorez," *Presence Africaine*, Paris.
Fanon, Frantz (1968) *The Wrethed of the Earth*, New York: Grove Press.
James, C.L.R. (1963), *The Black Jacobins*, New York: Vintage Books (Random House).
Maingot, Anthony P. (1979) "The Difficult Path to Socialism in the English–Speaking Caribbean" in Richard R. Fagen (ed) *Capitalism and the State in U.S. Latin*.
Mannheim, Karl (1953) "Conservative Thought" in Paul Kocskemeti, (ed) *Essays on Sociology and Social Psychology*, New York: Oxford University Press.
Ryan, Selwyn, Eddie Greene and Jack Harewood (1979), *The Confused Electorate* St. Augustine, Trinidad: ISER, UWI.

World Bank, (1978) *The Commonwealth Caribbean*, Baltimore: Johns Hopkins University Press.

BRIEF BIOGRAPHY

NAME	Anthony P. Maingot
DATE OF BIRTH	October 19 1937
ACADEMIC DEGREES	Ph.D. University of Florida, Gainesville 1967
	B.A. University of Florida, Gainesville, 1960
ACADEMIC AFFILIATIONS	Professor of Sociology Miami International University, Miami 1987 – Present
	Professor, Chairman, Department of Sociology-Anthropology, Florida International University, Miami Florida, 1976–1983
	Assistant Professor of Sociology and History, Yale University, New Haven, Connecticut, 1967–1972
BOOKS	*A Short History of the Caribbean* 4th ed., London: Macmillan, 1987 (Co-authors: Philip M. Sherlock and John H. Parry).
	The Military in Latin American Socio-Political Evolution, Washington, D.C.: Soro, American University, 1969 (Co-authors: Lyle N. McAlister and Robert Potash).

SELECTED ARTICLES

"Caribbean Society," in Tad Szulc (ed.), *The United States and the Caribbean*. The American Assembly of Columbia University. (New Jersey: Prentice Hall, Inc. 1971), pp 36-68

"National Sovereignty, Collective Security and the Realities of Power in the Caribbean Area," in Roy Preiswerk (ed.) *Regionalism and the Commonwealth Caribbean*. University of the West Indies, Trinidad, Institute of International Relations, 1969, pp 220-245

"From Ethnocentric to National History Writing in the Plural Society," *Caribbean Studies*, vol. 9, no. 3 (October 1969), pp 68-86

"Emigration and Development in the English-Speaking Caribbean, Working Paper No.6, Commission for the Study of International Migration and Cooperative Economic Development (Washington, D.C., July, 1989)

"Politics and Populist Historiography in the Caribbean," in Alistair Hennessy (ed.), *Currents in Caribbean Intellectual History* (Warwick University Caribbean Series), 1990

"United States Transnational Relations with the Caribbean," in Anthony Payne and Paul Sutton, *Caribbean Politics: A Comparative Analysis* (Manchester University Press), 1990

OTHER INFORMATION	Member of the Board of Contributors *The Miami Herald* (1981-present)
	Member of the Board of Directors, *Caribbean Affairs* (Trinidad)
	Sterring Committee, World Peace Foundation (Boston) Project on the Caribbean
	Editor, *Hemisphere*, A Magazine of Latin American and Caribbean Affairs, 1987-Present
	Specialist, Social Sciences, University of Puerto Rico, P.R. 1962

SECTION II

Strategies for Progress in the Post-Independence Caribbean: A Bradshawian Synthesis

S. B. JONES-HENDRICKSON

C. L. R. James carved scholarly acclaim for himself and heightened the fame of Toussaint L'Ouverture when, in the *Black Jacobins*, he developed the underpinnings of the power and leadership of Toussaint L'Ouverture. William Arthur Lewis, the 1979 Nobel Laureate in Economics, in a special *Social and Economic Studies* issue, December 1980 gave us a microscopically penetrating insight in the man who we call the Father of Caribbean Economics. Gordon Rohler (1981) stimulated us in *Pathfinder* and awoke us to the Black Awakening in the Arrivants of Edward Kamau Braithwaite, that man of letters and history. Within the last few months of 1983, Tim Hector fanned the flames of our understanding with some penetrating articles in his *Outlet* about Maurice Bishop. Archie Singham (1968) gave us a messianic and telescopic view of Matthew Eric Gairy. Ramesh Deosaran (1981) gave us a quick psychological assessment of the political leadership of Eric Williams: The man, his ideas and his politics. On another level, Edward Alpers and Pierre-Michelle Fontaine (1982) and others galvanized our understanding by succinctly taking us through Walter Rodney: *Revolutionary and Scholar: A Tribute*. We are grateful to these people for the understanding that they brought to the fore in our appreciating the nooks and crannies in the philosophical and psychological inner workings embodied in those people in question.

Over the years, there have been some political giants in the Eastern Caribbean microstates. In the large, these political giants' contributions to the political economic process have not been adequately catalogued or succinctly analyzed. We would have appreciated it if these people had given us their inward feelings in their own words. Failing that, we have to adopt a second-best solution and continue the tradition of those who assess the contributions of the people of the Caribbean.

One of the giants from the microstates economies was Robert Llewellyn Bradshaw of St. Kitts. Some Caribbean scholars scoffed at Michael Manley's books when they first appeared. For better or for worse, they are part of the literary landscape of Caribbean political economic issues. Bradshaw did not write any books. We have to assess his strategies for progress in the post-independence Caribbean from official documents, his speeches, our personal observations and impressions. We have dubbed our assessment a Bradshawian synthesis for the following reasons:

(1) we want to locate the contributions of Robert Bradshaw in a public choice perspective; and
(2) we want to anchor his contributions in a systemic ordering from a Rawlsian point of view.

The synthesis, therefore, pertains to the combination of various elements of his philosophical outlook that he attempted to bring together in a coherent whole.

After this introduction we will, schematically, discuss the Bradshawian synthesis from *five* points of coherence. Bradshaw as

(1) an architect of Caribbean integration;
(2) a principled, concerned, committed person;
(3) a champion of the working class;
(4) a self-sufficiency advocate; and
(5) finally, we will give a brief rationale for our highlighting the Bradshawian synthesis as a strategy for progress in the post-independence Caribbean.

Robert Llewellyn Bradshaw was born on September 16, 1916 in St. Paul's Village, St. Kitts. He died on May 23, 1978. Six years ago, this month, the man who was called Papa Bradshaw, the unofficial Father of St. Kitts-Nevis-Anguilla, ended forty years of politico-economic contributions to his country, the Caribbean and indeed the Third World. There is a morass of ambiguity, assertion, misunderstanding, travesty and truth surrounding Bradshaw's St. Kitts and St. Kitts's Bradshaw. Bradshaw has been called many things. Some of the things are true. But in the realm of veracity and accuracy, much is left to be desired in the bulk of the statements. Our purpose in this address is to unravel the complexity of his psychological and philosophical state and try to assess the essence of the man's contributions as strategies for progress in the post-independence Caribbean. In truth, however, our view must be one of "segmented reality" in words of Hal Blythe and Charlie Sweet.[1] We would be linking different points in his life to form a coherent whole. We are not merely interested in chronicling the history of Bradshaw's contributions. We are interested in the praxis of his contributions.

In evaluating Bradshaw, therefore, we echo Jim Snell (1983:38) who notes that an ". . . appreciation of history is a fundamental obligation, one which people in all times have accepted and discharged. By caring about and being moved by the person and deeds of our ancestors, we give assurance—and are assured—of a sort of immortality." We want to change this to say that our ancestors will be assured of some sort of immortality. The history of events is useful. But we are conscious of the maxim which forbids us from excavating the bones of the past on the grounds that the past is not the only place where reality exists. Reality, we recognize, also exists in the value space that we define and in which we define ourselves. Our motivation, as humans, lies in our system of values. Bradshaw had a strong motivation for change. His motivation was anchored to his system of values. He was a giant in a microstate with ideas that were filled with positive attributes for a macroscopic politico-economic post-independence Caribbean.

"History", Jacque Barzun contends, "is the realm in which the particular is the center of interest."[2] Bradshaw was the particular in the center of interest in the St. Kitts polity. His character is best understood by the concepts he held. He was not one to let sleeping dogmas sleep, nor was he one to give hazy doctrinal pronouncements. One thing that detailed his character and in a sense was central to the seemingly estranging features of the man, was the manner in which he attempted to extricate himself from the tyranny of the past and established himself as an architect of Caribbean integration.

AN ARCHITECT OF CARIBBEAN INTEGRATION

If we abstract from the hypocrisy of the time, and if we impound in ceteris paribus some of the self-serving tales of rhetorical grandstanding of the political directorate, we can still conclude from the telegrams sent to St. Kitts on Bradshaw's death that the man was an architect of Caribbean integration. Michael Manley, former Prime Minister of

Jamaica, saw him as "an eminent West Indian statesman and leader whose contributions to Caribbean unity will always be remembered . . ."[3] Bradshaw had a vision of a United Caribbean. He was one of the many key architects of the West Indies Federation, and served with distinction in the Federal Government as Minister of Finance. According to Vere Bird, Senior, Prime Minister of Antigua, Bradshaw played "an important role in trying to educate both the people and the leaders of this region about the value of a united Caribbean . . ." Austin Bramble, former Chief Minister of Montserrat, said that Bradshaw's "understanding of the Caribbean and its people was outstanding and his vision and unswerving dedication to a Caribbean in which all the people enjoyed happiness and security as a result of unity and cooperation were infectious."

In some respects, these statements could be seen as sound words that may not be easily condemned—to paraphrase the *Labour Spokesman*, the organ of the St. Kitts-Nevis-Anguilla Labour Party.

It is easy to understand Bradshaw as an architect of Caribbean integration and, in train, deduce from this characteristic an activism that expressed itself as a strategy for progress in the post-independence Caribbean. From the evaluations of his political contemporaries, as well as our observations of the man and his actions, it is clear that he had a powerful penchant for unity. He expressed his aversion for fragmentation so often that, in the Aristotelian sense, "that which was expressed was impressed" (Harris, 1973:50) on the minds of Caribbean people. But for many, there were several episodes of knife-stabbing discoveries vis-a-vis his position on integration.

One such episode took place between July 25–31, 1976, at the Commonwealth Caribbean Conference on Anguilla which was held in Barbados. Bradshaw was being pressured to let Anguilla go. He refused to budge on the issue. Instead he opted for giving Nevis and Anguilla the essentiality of more local government (Prieswerk, 1970:827). This may be interpreted as intransigence or dictatorship. If it were intransigence, it was intransigence in a sense that the state had to stay together. The people had to run their own affairs and forget the idea of blaming others for their shortcomings. This view is evident from his Statehood Day Address at Warner Park, February, 1974:

> We won't manage by lamentation. Nor indeed would we manage by assigning blame, particularly to our external tormentors, because that would be wasted effort.
>
> We will manage only by recognizing what our situation is, by identifying the tools and resources available to us, by truly uniting ourselves and by working as a nation, albeit, an embryonic one, to ameliorate, if not overcome, our present difficulties.
>
> Disunity and destructiveness are luxuries that this country cannot now or in the foreseeable future afford.

If it were dictatorship, it was dictatorship that he thought was necessary to cement a common bond among Caribbean people at the microstate level of St. Kitts-Nevis-Anguilla and at the macrostate level of a Caribbean Nation State. The bond of integration was necessary in light of the attitudinal frame of reference of West Indians in destroying their own. This view is clear from his 1973 Statehood Day Address at Grove Park, Nevis:

> The West Indies have a failing of creating difficulties for themselves, the greatest evidence of this being demolition of the carefully constructed West Indies Federation in 1962. Had the Federation been allowed to live, we could as one nation already have been a single common community . . . We are paying dearly for the mistakes of 1962. But, for the sake of our

succeeding generation, it is ardently hoped that we able to formulate a happy issue out of our difficulties . . .

A second episode of his pro-integration, anti-fragmentation stance was his July 26, 1974 position on signing the CARICOM Treaty in Jamaica. Britain and some Caribbean governments were attempting to pressure Bradshaw to sign the Treaty of Chaguaramas on behalf of St. Kitts and Nevis. In April 1974 the British advised him that he should sign for St. Kitts and Nevis since Anguilla was, technically, under Britain's jurisdiction. Bradshaw made his point with remarkable skill and tenacity. He signed the Treaty as the twelfth member of the Caribbean Community and Common Market. And he let Britain know, in no uncertain terms, that he considered the United Kingdom's advice "inappropriate and unacceptable."

Bradshaw sought to maintain the integrity of CARICOM. He saw CARICOM as the vehicle that will keep the region's people together. In his July 15, 1974 address to the Opening Session of the CARICOM Heads of Government, he said:

> . . . CARICOM will exert a growing influence upon the lives of its people although they are located over vast expanses of sea and land. That influence will be an amalgam of attitude, of thought, of economies, and of psychology, that together should truly liberate us, making us feel less as trespassers and more as participants in the world scene. In a word, CARICOM will provide the dynamic to propel the new Caribbean man.

This last observation is an embodiment of Bradshaw the man as an architect of Caribbean integration. Implicit in his view, also, is his strategies for progress in the post-independence Caribbean: "an amalgam of attitude, thought, economics, psychology . . .;" in essence "the dynamic to propel the new Caribbean man." Carlos A. Downing, editor of Tortola's *The Island Sun* captured the strength of Bradshaw's philosophy as an architect of Caribbean integration when he editorialized on Bradshaw's death in the June 3, (1978:11) issue:

> ... Premier Bradshaw was a store house of energy which was felt not only in the Associated State where his voice was honey to the masses, but throughout the Caribbean. He was a West Indian first and last, and his dream in seeing a federated West Indies as an autonomous Nation never wavered. When the first attempt . . . failed . . . Mr. Bradshaw was the most depressed advocate. Almost singularly he kept the flame burning.

Bradshaw kept the flames of Caribbean integration and anti-fragmentation aloft. The flames were kept burning at the state level in St. Kitts-Nevis and Anguilla and at the regional level of the Caribbean Nation State. In his pursuit of both objectives, Bradshaw was a politician of regionalism and nationalism. His nationalism is readily seen in his principles, concerns and commitment.

A MAN OF PRINCIPLES, CONCERN AND COMMITMENT

Our view of Bradshaw as a nationalist is couched within the matrix of his principles, concern and commitment to the state of St. Kitts-Nevis-Anguilla. That he was a regionalist and nationalist at the same time may seem paradoxical. This was the nature of the man. At another level of conceptualization, however, this dual characteristic was not paradoxical if one understands the tenets of nationalism under which we view Bradshaw.

According to John Breuilly (1982:2): ". . . nationalism is, above and beyond all else, about politics, and . . . politics is about power. Power, in the modern world, is primarily about control of state." In our view, one of Bradshaw's principles centered on this issue of nationalism. For him, in our view, the nationalist argument is a political construct based on three key assertions:

(a) There exists a nation with an explicit and peculiar character.
(b) The interests and values of this nation take priority over all other interests and values.
(c) The nation must be as independent as possible. This usually requires at least the attainment of political sovereignty (Breuilly, 1982:3).

Bradshaw's principles of nationalism were embodied in power. It was not power in a stark dictatorial sense or crass materialistic purview. It was nationalist power in the way Marilyn Abbey defines power. "Power", she contends, "is the capacity or ability to get things done — to exercise control over other people, events and oneself" (Abbey, 1981:37). Whenever he got the opportunity, Bradshaw reminded the people of the past and the present: what was and what is. In a Samuelsonian sense, Bradshaw was mindful of the notion that "one interested in fruitful statics must study dynamics" (Samuelson, 1970:5). He understood the static world of the state and the region. Furthermore, he recognized that the political economy of the state and the region was in continual revision. Since he saw himself as a member of an enlightened political directorate, he perceived of his goal as one of putting St. Kitts-Nevis and Anguilla first, and the region second. The priority, however, did not undermine his principles to both entities.

Bradshaw was apparently always concerned that he not be

dictated to from abroad. He saw himself as capable as, if not more than, the British overlords to whom he had to submit colonial reports. This concern, too, was a paradox as we will observe in the section on champion of the working class. We will cite two examples to illustrate his concern that the views from abroad not be the dominant position on the direction of development in St. Kitts-Nevis-Anguilla.

First, in July 1950, there was a new move towards self-government in the Windward and Leeward Islands. Bradshaw strenuously opposed the British Secretary of State's point relative to the mode and method of operations. He was against the idea that Britain planned to implement. He saw, in the idea of political organization, a system that would have deprived him and his Labour Party of total control of the elected segment of the Presidency of the Legislative Council. Bradshaw wanted to command a power position through a legislative quorum. This was a strong concern and principle entwined. Bradshaw lost on this principle and concern. The change came about since the Crown used its reserved powers to thwart what was perceived by the British as Bradshaw's obstinacy. It is safe to say, nonetheless, that Bradshaw must have come to grips with the salience of the problem, and temporarily permitted himself to be seduced by the paraphernalia of British authority.

A second case which revolves around Bradshaw's question of concern stems from the arrogance of the British in their treatment of colonials. In October 1950, Bradshaw was the key leader who led a mammoth demonstration in Basseterre to protest the Colonial Office high-handed manner in the appointment of Governors and Administrators in the Caribbean colonies. This demonstration, codenamed, "Operation Blackburne," was another reminder to the British overlords that their wishes were not to be the only weights of authority in St. Kitts-Nevis-Anguilla.

A third issue which pertains to the concern of Bradshaw

occurred in 1949. At the formation of a new trade union in November 1949, at County Hall, London, Bradshaw and the other union leaders were all fundamentally concerned about the programs of the new union. They wanted the union to focus on attacking unemployment and hiking the standards and levels of living in the peripheral capitalist economies in which their leaders lived. Many of the leaders wanted strong trade unions and sound economic policies to avert what they call totalitarianism in the Caribbean. Bradshaw was very forceful in this regard. He said:

> For the information of the Conference and the Congress which will spring from its womb shortly, I would tell you that the Communists of Great Britain have now turned their attention to the West Indies. They have been issuing a cyclostyled journal. Up to the time when I left my island only the third copy was out, in which they pretend to champion the cause of the West Indian workers. You will see, therefore, that these malignant microbes are not all idle, and like the roots of trees searching for food, they are ever on the alert to find grounds filled with manure suitable for their growth." (Free World Congress, *Official Report*, 1949; Hoyos, 1974:163).

That was a remarkable concern. It was a concern, however, woven in the fabric of a David Hume-type philosophy. David Hume in his essay, *Treatise of Human Nature*, more than 200 years ago, "showed that truths of reason are true by definition, like mathematical axioms, but that the truths of the world in which we live are based on experience instead of logic." (Branch, 1977:14). Bradshaw was echoing the sentiments of Caribbean leaders such as G. L. F. Charles and Carl La Corbiniere of St. Lucia and Grantley Adams of Barbados. His forceful concern was not to be daunted even though he was firmly aware of the views of the four H's of Jamaica: Ken

Hill, Richard Hart, Frank Hill and Arthur Henry. Bradshaw recognised that he lived in a world in which experience and not logic had to dictate his modus operandi. In a metaphysical sense, his concern about the role of communists in the Caribbean Labor Movement was based on our view of him as a reductionistic and holistic politician. As a reductionist, his preference was a concentration on the mechanisms and components of the Labor Movement in his St. Kitts-Nevis-Anguilla. As a holistic politician, he recognized that he had to focus on the Caribbean labor, organically as a whole organism. In other words, if the philosophy of Britian's "malignant microbes" were planted in the Caribbean labor movement, his labor movement in St. Kitts-Nevis-Anguilla would be in jeopardy, and in train his power base would be destroyed. For him, therefore, the truth of the role of communism in the Caribbean Labor Movement was not something which emerged on the political altar at a trade union meeting in London. Rather, it was a truth which had to be bound in the dynamics of the political system at the country level. And for him, in his country, he wanted nothing to do with communists. This, however, is another of the paradoxical feature of the man. It was the Labor Party of St. Kitts-Nevis-Anguilla which made "Comrade" part of the political lexicon when I was a young man growing up in Sandy Point. In a true enigmatic role, in 1975, it was Bradshaw's Labor Party that likened itself to a socialist government (SKNALP. Manifesto, 1975:18).

The last part of the trilogy of this section is commitment. To state that Bradshaw was a leader is make a commentary on the obvious. His leadership centered on his commitment and credibility. His credibility was the core of his communication. In his commitment and credibility scenario, one political comment looms large as questioning his commitment to all of the people of St. Kitts-Nevis-Anguilla. The communication is the allegation that was attributed to him, namely, that he would put "bones in the rice of Nevisians and pepper in the soup of Anguillians," ostensibly to deter their fragmenting the state of St. Kitts-Nevis-Anguilla.

We say allegation because many of the torch bearers of this statement have a symptomatic similarity to those people who C. L. R. James (1977:73) describes as ". . . the worshippers at the shrine of myth . . ." Whether we believe the statement to be or not to be myth is not material at this stage. What is material is our trying to understand the essence of the statement and deduce from it, if possible, the salience of a strategy for preventing a state from fragmenting.

In many respects, people recover from the symptoms of a saying; seldom do they recover from the label associated with the saying. Bradshaw's commitment may not recover, adequately, from the syndrome associated to the "bones in the rice, pepper in the soup" statement. It took a certain "effort of will," in the Bertrand Russell (1967) sense for him to have made such a statement. Bradshaw epitomised the substance of the Labor Party commitment ". . . to provide a community framework within which every man, woman and child (in St. Kitts-Nevis-Anguilla) . . . find full scope for the development of his of her individuality but, at the same time, within which the essential equality of all people (is) recognized and respected." (SKNALP, Manifesto, 1975:18).

If we accept this guiding philosophy as more than a murky doctrinal rhetoric, then we have to seek to understand Bradshaw and Bradshawianism in another light. We have to see him within the swirling nexus of events which may have caused him to make such a statement.

In trying to understand Bradshaw and Bradshawianism, we have to go beyond the facts surrounding the nature of the man. We have to understand the nature of the facts surrounding the human predicament of the man. This is the canvas against which we have to understand him and his statement. Bradshaw had a commitment to ensure that his actions permitted the possibility of positive change in the state. He saw himself as having the responsibility to apply his observations of what he thought ought to be the remedy for preserving the integrity of the state. In a perverse sense, therefore, this may have been the motivation for the "bones in the rice, pepper in the soup" statement. The idea of fragmentation was so nauseating to him that he may have played out of character to achieve unity.

In the final analysis, the *substance* in this "bones in the rice, pepper in the soup" statement must be paradoxical and false. The statement would be true, logically, if and only if it were false since Bradshaw's life and Bradshawianism was steeped in a Rawlsian system of justice. The essence of the falsehood and the paradox is not merely a trivial feedback in semantics. The numbing finality of the statement must be clearly paradoxical, if the man believed in equality and equity, as the evidence indicates that he did. Like Copernicus' heliocentric theory of the solar system, this "bones in the rice, pepper in the soup" statement has remained central to the magnets of repulsion vis-a-vis Bradshaw's commitment to equality and justice for Kittitians, Nevisians and Anguillians.

Bradshaw's determination was infused with an irresistible enthusiasm. He had an unusual sensitivity to important events and an uncanny ability to make the right move at the right time, and make the appropriate comment at the appropriate time. He saw a recurring need for integrity and commitment in his fathering the state of St. Kitts-Nevis-Anguilla to nationhood. In this case of "bones in the rice, pepper in the soup," however, Bradshaw may have killed the right process with the wrong procedure. In a manner of analysis, therefore, Bradshaw must have recognized that the secessionist sentiments in Nevis and Anguilla would ultimately take both islands away from his control; so his "bones in the rice, pepper in the soup" was what Walter Rodney (1981:220) would term ". . . a sort of irrendist pressure . . ." on Nevis and Anguilla. Labor's base was and is in St. Kitts. But the working class was in all three islands. He wanted to remain committed to the integrity of the state and the working class.

CHAMPION OF THE WORKING CLASS

Bradshawianism and Bradshaw as a philosophy and a man oriented to the working class may be securely anchored in the seven-week strike of April to May, 1940. Through the St. Kitts Workers League, subsequently renamed the St. Kitts-Nevis-Anguilla Labor Party, Bradshaw was to catapult his philosophy of a theory of social justice for the working class in St. Kitts-Nevis-Anguilla. The seven-week strike of 1940 was a precursor to the thirteen-week strike of 1948. Bradshaw was almost nineteen in January 1935 when there was a general strike of agricultural workers in St. Kitts. When a group of workers went to an estate to demand higher wages from the owner, the owner opened fire on them, wounding three persons. This heightened the affair. When police arrived, they were unable to control the crowd. They too opened fire on the crowd, killing three and wounding eight. The police, supplemented by a British warship, broke the back of the strike and strikers. Wages and working conditions were not improved. This sporadic, leaderless strike left a bitter experience among the dejected workers. The strike in St. Kitts, however, had two impacts: first, it was the catalyst for a series of strikes that engulfed the entire Caribbean as Sir W. Arthur Lewis (1977) has so adequately depicted; second, it served as the crux of Bradshaw's determination to work on behalf of the working class. That measure was fortified by the fact that he himself was from the working class and the sugar belt of St. Paul's.

Long before John Rawl's *A Theory of Justice* was published in 1971, Bradshaw was concerned with the spirit and substance of societal obligation endemic in what may be termed Rawlsian philosophy. Rawls contends that "justice is the first virtue of social institutions." The "Rawlsian Difference Principle" states that "justice is realized when social and economic inequalities have been arranged so that their differences yield the greatest satisfaction to the least disadvantaged without reducing the satisfaction of anyone" (Spencer, 1980:59).

The rule deriving from Rawlsian principle is this: "Any social action should be undertaken if it will make the least advantaged person better off without making anyone worse off" (Spencer, 1980:59). Rawls argues that the adherence to this guideline improves equity. The equity is improved when "those who have been favored by nature with talent, wealth, or other social advantage may gain from their good fortune only when it improves those who had lost out". (Spencer, 1980:59). This spirit of equity and the Rawlsian principle of justice underpinned Bradshaw's rationale for the acquisition of the sugar lands and assets of the St. Kitts (Basseterre) Sugar Factory, Limited. In this one act, we see the paramountcy of the man's leadership in institutionalizing his role as champion of the working class.

St. Kitts is a pure plantation economy. The fortunes of St. Kitts are inextricably linked to the fortunes of sugar. Bradshaw derived his power base from sugar. Beginning in 1952 when the need for public control of the sugar industry was raised (*Background*, 1976:2), the Bradshaw government and Labor Party were always on the lookout for acquiring the sugar industry. When the acquisition presented itself in 1969, later to be consummated in an agreement on December 13, 1976, the Government of Robert Bradshaw had truly positioned itself as advocate of working class rights. Bradshaw's final chapter in the long struggle against the plantocracy was ended.

In a statement read by the then Attorney General, Lee L. Moore, in October, Bradshaw hinted to the plantocracy his mood about the sugar industry. He said: ". . . the ingenious form of the joint stock company is such as to render it immortal, and thus to make unending the apparent rights of shareholders to a part of the surplus produced by the sweat and toil of the workers of St. Kitts" (Jamaica *Daily News*, October 17, 1967:4). ". . . You have made enough, you have had had your fill, and your investment has been most rewarding . . . You have made enough. If you are genuinely seeking agreement, do not press for what is unreasonable. The Government will not, and cannot depart from the principles I have encountered, because to do so would be to betray our responsibilities to generations of workers of this island—and that we will never do" (Jamaica *Daily News*, 1976:4). Bradshaw's government had rescued the sugar industry in 1972 from what Bradshaw characterized as an "extremely critical point where, as it were, (the sugar industry) had one foot in the grave and the other on a piece of ripe banana skin" (SKNA *Newsletter*, 1975: Vol. 4, No. 4:3).

The rescue of the sugar industry and the subsequent acquisition of the sugar industry, despite *present conundrums* to the contrary, meant that Bradshaw had placed a stamp of approval on an issue, to wit, "that the sugar lands of St. Kitts shall forever remain public property" (St. Kitts-Nevis-Anguilla *Newsletters*, 1975: Vol. 5 No. 4:5). He had secured his power base. He had, within the vortex of antagonistic relations emanating from the plantocracy, made the workers of St. Kitts the beneficiaries of the first state in the economic space of the country. And in a causally linked fashion he had, once again, heightened the politicization of the working class nexus into a base of popular support and power wherein he and the Labor Party would dominate the politico-economic issues in St. Kitts-Nevis-Anguilla.

Salimu in an "Outlet Essay" (*Outlet*, January 13, 1984:2) characterized C. L. R. James of *Beyond a Boundary* fame as a person:

> Unswerving in his optimism about the working class as the motive force of change in the Caribbean and the world. (James believed that Caribbean people have it within them to) challenge the hypocrisy and oppression when the rules of the game at one level of society contradict the rules of the game in the working class world.

Salimu called this view Jamesian. It is vintage Bradshawian philosophy and synthesis, in our view. And the acquisition of the sugar industry in 1976 was a classic testimony to the philosophy of Bradshaw that, once again, imprinted him on the consciousness of the working class and reinforced the sobriquent, "Papa Bradshaw – the champion of the working class."

Within the critical conjuncture of forces that made Bradshaw a champion of the working class and an anti-plantocracy advocate was his paradoxical predilection for things British. Bradshaw seemed British to the core. But, in his multifaceted manner, the philosophy of Bradshawianism that guided him was African-based. Bradshaw regarded the colonial past as one of exploitation and humiliation. He, therefore, strove to articulate a procedure of development that was oriented to the basic needs of the working class. Unlike George Beckford (1972), Paul Baran (1975), Andre Gunder Frank (1975) or Walter Rodyney (1974), he never viewed Western economic history as irrelevant to the development trajectories of developing countries: In:

(1) his government's acquisition of the sugar lands of St. Kitts;
(2) the upliftment of St. Kitts and Nevis from the days of "chigger-foot" and yaws;
(3) the bringing home to St. Kitts sons of the soil who were considered derelicts in Santo Domingo.

he was for his people. In all of these instances he was attempting to inject a sense of pride and power in the working-class of St. Kitts. He was in a sense convincing the people that one of their strategies for progress in the post-independence St. Kitts-Nevis-Anguilla was for them to be creators of circumstances rather than creatures of circumstances.

Amidst all of this positive working class, labor power thrust, Bradshaw remained particularly anglophone in deportment. But central to his British mannerisms, however, was his concern with the interactions of economic and political domination in the world, particularly the Third World. His close links with Papa Doc of Haiti was born not of the tragedy endemic in the Haitian politico-economic structure under the Papa Doc in his last years, but in the glorious past that was Haiti's when men like Toussaint L'Ouverture, Henri Christophe and the young Duvalier charted strategies for progress in the post-independence era of their country.

Bradshaw's main British-traits were his style of dress and manner of speaking. Yet we feel confident to contend that Bradshaw must have concluded, long before Michael Korda (1977) and John Malloy made it popular, to "dress for success." On occasions he may also have invoked the Norman Manley injunction, namely:

> We can take everything the English education has to offer us but ultimately we must reject the domination of her influence, because we are not English nor should we ever want to

be. Instead we must dig deep into our own consciousness and accept and reject only those things of which we from our superior knowledge of our cultural needs must be the best judges (Manley in Nettleford, 1971:109; Nettleford, 1978: 67–68).

It is our view that Bradshaw's preference for things British was not in the bankrupt Naipaulian sense of a mimic man, but rather Bradshaw had a penchant for pricking the pretensions of the British. While his anglophone traits may have been center stage at times, as champion of the working class he seemed consistently conscious of the power of labor. While he may not have put it like John Eaton (1966:7), he would have agreed that the "process of production—the labor process—is the process by which labor converts the material supplied by nature into wealth, the process of changing nature to serve the needs of man." When Bradshaw is viewed as champion of the working class and master mind of the sugar industry acquisition, his paradoxical trait assumes a third order of importance. Workers had to be self-sufficient in a post-independence St. Kitts-Nevis-Anguilla and the wider Caribbean.

A SELF-SUFFICIENCY ADVOCATE

The English philosopher and mathematician, Sir Isaac Newton, is credited with having pointed out in 1687 that "for every action there is an equal and opposite reaction." Bradshaw's philosophical expression which we are calling Bradshawianism was one such action that brought opposite reaction. This did not daunt his spirits. In his last speech in the House of Assembly, 1977, he said:

STRATEGIES FOR PROGRESS IN POST-INDEPENDENCE 141

In looking ahead, Mr. Speaker, and we must perforce look ahead if we're not to attract Goeth's rebuke:

'They know not witherward they're wending because they have not looked ahead'

In looking ahead, therefore, we shall have at least to take account of the profound political and economic state of the world in which terrible violence plays so great a part; of the deteriorating and ruinous energy crisis; of the insecurity of our regional institutions; of our international insignificance; of the marginal nature and falling volume of our production; and, above all, of the need actively to be seen to be helping ourselves. (Budget Address, Minister of Finance, December, 1977).

This concept of "to be seen to be helping ourselves" was long enshrined in Bradshawianism as a strategy for progress in post-independence St. Kitts-Nevis-Anguilla. In the 1950's, St. Kitts-Nevis-Anguilla was the only territory of the Eastern Caribbean that did not accept grant-in-aid from Britain— "grant-in-aid" that Gordon Lewis (1968:12) so aptly described as having "concomitant humiliating surveillance of daily expenditures by the United Kingdom Treasury." This strategy for progress in post-independence St. Kitts-Nevis-Anguilla was critical to Bradshaw because he recognized that, despite political independence, the Caribbean countries still did not disentangle themselves from the tentacles of European and North American influence and dominance. Bradshaw, therefore, attempted to create in St. Kitts-Nevis-Anguilla a system that permitted him to integrate his views in the social fabric of the islands. Self-reliance, to him, depended on the internal resources of his state and he saw this as a strategy to be institutionalized by the entire Caribbean. He made his view known in no uncertain terms.

On June 15, 1975 when he was addressing a one-day conference of Finance Ministers of the Associated States,

Grenada and Montserrat, he said: "Our great trouble is simply that we are living beyond our means by relentlessly trying to sustain a standard of life which cannot be supported by our falling agricultural production." (The Jamaica *Daily News*, June 4, 1975:4). This is nothing more than what many of us have been saying, that we in the Caribbean are trying to sustain caviar taste on saltfish income. This view was not an academic view that suddenly was incorporated in Bradshawianism. Bradshaw tried to keep the idea of self-sufficiency and the strategies for post-independence ever present in the minds of his people.

In delivering his Statehood Day Broadcast, February, 1976 he emphasized the themes of self-sufficiency in terms of what it would be when independence arrived:

> To be independent means that you neither depend upon nor are subordinated to anyone. Thus, as we approach the Independence which we have freely and deliberately decreed for ourselves, let us be in no doubt at all about that which we shall embark upon, for manna will not fall from heaven just like that. Let us face it knowing that it will demand of us hard work, patriotism, dedication, denial, objectivity, unity and self-respect, and we must continue to be seen actively to be helping ourselves.

In this view is Bradshawianism at its zenith. Bradshaw, however, was mindful of the Rawlsian system of justice. He recognized that benefits had to be shifted from Peter to Paul — from the plantocracy to the masses. His guiding light, however, was the importance he placed on self-sufficiency and respect for race. In an address at a West Indian Solidarity Conference in St. Thomas, U.S. Virgin Islands, January 13, 1973 he stated:

I assert that the Negro possesses total political power in the Commonwealth Caribbean and in Haiti, at least; but he needs economic strength with which to buttress, sustain and support that power if he is ever to attain the equality he so ardently seeks.

That economic strength will be gained neither by shouting slogans, waving banners, nor indeed by being truculent and offensive. It will be gained only upon the basis of hard work, particularly by our youth; objective education at the highest level; systematic planning for the future; and above all realistic unity among the various Negro peoples of the Caribbean, coupled with an ever-deepening love of himself by the Negro in the West Indies as a race.

Bradshaw had no illusions that these ideas, which we are calling Bradshawianism, would be implemented without reaction and with ease. His philosophy was critical to the survival of the masses in the Caribbean. He seemed fully aware of the temperament of the Caribbean political directorate when it comes to their making a decision. On this score, he blasted his fellow leaders on this concept of indecision on October 31, 1976, after the October 6 Cubana destruction off the coast of Barbados. In speaking in the House of Assembly he said, "Pertinent happenings after the crash do not speak well for resoluteness. They have shown up once again . . . that when the hard crunch of decision-making strikes West Indians, we duck and hedge and vacillate."

STRATEGIES FOR PROGRESS

In the final analysis, the centerfold of politico-economic development in St. Kitts-Nevis-Anguilla during the Bradshaw era was Bradshawianism—a nationalist articulation of strategies for progress which were not bound by the state of St. Kitts-Nevis-Anguilla. Our passion for the truth of Bradshawianism must be silenced by the weight of the undisputed authority of the evidence surrounding the implementation of Bradshaw's philosophy. The critical dynamic of his philosophy was his impulse to maintain unity at all costs in three distinct islands, or as Albert Gomes terms them in *Through A maze of Colour*, "A freak of recent Colonial Office Constitutional gimmickry" (Gomes, 1976:22). Bradshaw's insistence on maintaining territorial integrity of this 'freak of British Colonial Office gimmickry' placed him in the light of a dictator. Some evaluators, therefore, saw symbols of his philosophy but were blinded by the substance. As a result of his alleged dictatorship, "he was much traduced and maligned" (Gomes, 1976:22).

In the final analysis, our fundamental aim in assessing Bradshawianism was to show that Bradshaw viewed history as handmaiden of the people of St. Kitts-Nevis-Anguilla from the perspective of what was achieved and could be created by self-respect and self-reliance. We could be indicted for oversimplication as we attempt to draw the relevant strategies for progress in the post-independence Caribbean from the philosophy of Bradshaw alone. His work was complemented with the strength of the other stalwarts of the St. Kitts-Nevis-Labour Party. But to paraphrase C. L. R. James speaking about Toussaint L'Ouverture, Bradshaw dominated St. Kitts-Nevis-Anguilla from his entry until death removed him from the scene. Except for his short stint as first Minister of Finance of the West Indies Federation, the history of St. Kitts-Nevis-Anguilla between 1940–1978, is the historical manifestation of Bradshawianism.

We believe that the history of the microstate of St. Kitts-Nevis-Anguilla between 1940–1978 has solid pointers as strategies for progress in the post-independence Caribbean.

Two comments are appropriate, nevertheless, about this historical citation. First, those who ignore the past are like drowning philosophers who are arguing about specific gravity of their bodies and wetness of the water in which they are drowning; or they are like half-baked physicists-pilots who are debating the merits of Bernoulli's Principle when their plane is crashing. We cannot remain anchored to the past or mired in our conceits. We have to make continual evaluations of our location in space and time. We have to know where we came from and where we plan to go. This is the essence of Bradshawianism. It is a philosophy that understood where the working class of the Caribbean came from, and where they are capable of going with discipline. It, therefore, is a philosophy that is not set specific to St. Kitts-Nevis-Anguila.

Second, our rationale in selecting Bradshaw and his philosophy was to raise, to a higher level, the consciousness of Caribbean scholars of the contributions of leaders in the microstates of the Caribbean. Too often, the Caribbean, its leadership and its philosophy are circumscribed in the ambit of the so-called MDCs—although all could be properly called LDCs. In generating macropolitical strategies from a microstate case study, we are, however, mindful of Patrick Emmanuel's (1981:131) comments that "the approaches to the comparative study of Caribbean politics" must be one in which there are linkages to the global concepts of political economy that is dependency and political sociology, that is the social class system. We believe that Bradshawianism is a dynamic thrust in this area. While it is one case study, the bases for comparisons are all over the microstates of the Eastern Caribbean.

Vaughan A. Lewis, the most active present-day Caribbean integrationist, captures the substance of the Bradshawian synthesis when he said:

> When the weight of colonial authority and its administrative system is removed from any society . . . the opportunity arises for the first time for the component elements of the society to make . . . decisions . . . (about) the sets of arrangements . . . that they can undertake among themselves to ensure the society's persistence and development (Lewis, 1976:340).

It is our firmly held view that the Bradshawian synthesis was geared to an articulation of such a persistence and development. In sum, when we assess Bradshawianism in light of strategies for progress in the post-independence Caribbean, we should not be preoccupied with the physiognomy of the philosophy; instead, we must be concerned with the physiology and the ideological frame of reference from which Bradshawianism stems. Bradshawianism or the Bradshawian synthesis is one conjuncture of forces that was aimed at ensuring that in the post-independence Caribbean, the people must be real creators of circumstances rather than creatures of constraints. It is a philosophy to which all of us as Caribbean people and scholars should subscribe.

NOTES

1. See Blythe and Sweet (1984) for a useful development of this concept.
2. Cited in Cole's (1983:7)
3. All of the quotations from Bradshaw, except where otherwise noted, were taken from *Robert Llewellyn Bradshaw, 1916-1978*. (The memorial booklet and order of burial service, 1978).

REFERENCES

Abbey, Marilyn, R. (1981) "The Art of Negotiation." *Success*, (February) 34-41.

Alpers, Edward A. and Pierre-Michel Fontaine, (1982) (eds.) *Walter*

Rodney: Revolutionary and Scholar A Tribute Los Angeles: Center for Afro-American Studies and African Studies Center, UCLA

Baran, Paul A. (1957) *Political Economy of Growth* New York: Monthly Review Press.

Barzan, Jacque (1983) *A Stroll with William James*. New York: Harper and Row.

Beckford, George L. (1972) *Persistent Poverty: Underdevelopment in Plantation Economics of the Third World*. New York: Oxford University Press.

Blythe, Hal and Charlie Sweet (1984) "The Right Way to Write about what you know." *Writer's Digest*, (April) 25-27

Branch, Taylor (1977) "New Frontiers in American Philosophy." *The New York Times Magazine*. (August 14): 14

Breuilly, John (1982) *Nationalism and the State*. New York: St. Martin's Press.

Coles, Robert. (1983) "A Passionate Commitment to Experience" *The New York Times Book Review*. (May 29) :7

Deosaran, Ramesh (1981) *Eric Williams: The Man, His Ideas and His Politics*, Port-of-Spain, Trinidad: Signum Publishing Company.

Downing, Carlos (1978) "Premier Bradshaw has left Indelible Mark" *The Island Sun*. (Editorial), (June 3)

Eaton, John (1966) *Political Economy* New York: International Publishers.

Emmanuel, Patrick (1981) "Approaches to the Comparative Study of Caribbean Politics: Some Comments," *Social and Economic Studies*, 30: 119-136.

Frank, Andre Gunder (1957) *Capitalism and Underdevelopment in Latin America*, New York: Monthly Review Press.

Gomes, Albert (1976) "Through a Maze of Colour." *The Sunday Gleaner Magazine*, (February 22):3

Harris, Thomas A. (1973) *I'm Ok—You're Ok*, New York: Avon Publishers.

Hoyos, F. A. (1974) *Grantley Adams and the Social Revolution* London: MacMillan.

James, C. L. R. (1963) *The Black Jacobins: Toussaint-L'Ouverture and*

the Santo Domingo Revolution. Wesport, Conn: Lawrence Hill Company.
Jamaica *Daily News.* (1976) "You have made enough St. Kitts tells Sugar Company." (October 17).
Jamaica *Daily News* (1975) "Caribbean People living beyond their means: Bradshaw." (June 16).
Lewis, W. Arthur (1980) "Biological Note," *Social and Economic Studies,* (Special Issue) 29, 4.
Lewis, W. Arthur (1977) *Labour in the West Indies* (with afterword by Susan Craig), London: New Beacon Books.
Lewis, Gordon (1968) *The Growth of the Modern West Indies.* New York: Monthly Review Press.
Lewis, Vaughan A. (1976) *Size, Self-Determination and International Relations: The Caribbean.* Kingston: Institute of Social and Economic Research, UWI.
Korda, Michael (1977) *Success.* New York: Random House.
Nettleford, Rex (1971) *Manley and the New Jamaica,* London: Longman Caribbean.
Nettleford, Rex (1978) *Caribbean Cultural Identity: The Case of Jamaica.* Kingston: Institute of Jamaica
Prieswerk, Roy (ed) (1970) "Conflicts and Disputes" in *Documents on International Relations in the Caribbean,* Puerto Rico: Institute of Caribbean Studies U.P.R.
Rawls, John (1971) *A Theory of Justice* Mass: Harvard University Press
Rodney, Walter (1974) *How Europe Underdeveloped Africa.* Washington: Howard University Press.
Rodney, Walter (1981) *A History of the Guyanese Working People, 1981-1905* Baltimore: The John Hopkins University Press.
Rohler, Gordon, *Pathfinder,* Port-of-Spain, Trinidad: The College Press.
Stone, Carl (1986) *Class, State and Democracy in Jamaica* New York: Praeger Publishers.

BRIEF BIOGRAPHY

NAME	S. B. Jones-Hendrickson
DATE OF BIRTH	June 3, 1945
ACADEMIC DEGREES	Ph.D. 1976 University of Exeter, Devon England, (Economics)
	M.S. 1970 Illinois State University, Normal Illinois (Economics)
	B.S. 1969 Illinois State University, Normal Illinois (Economics)
	A.A. College of the Virgin Islands St. Thomas, USVI, 1967
ACADEMIC AFFILIATIONS	Professor of Economics, University of The Virgin Islands, 1990
	Associate Professor of Economics, CVI, UVI 1982-1990
	Assistant Professor at the University of the Virgin Islands 1976-1982
	Lecturer University of the West Indies 1973-1976
BOOKS	*Readings in Caribbean Public Sector Economics*, Institute of Social and Economic Research, University of the West Indies, Jamaica, 1981 (Co-edited with Fuat Andic)
	Public Finance and Monetary Policy in Open Economies, Institute of Social and

Economic Research, University of the West Indies, Jamaica, 1985

Interviews with Lee L. Moore: (Editor), Eastern Caribbean Institute, Frederiksted, USVI, 1988

SELECTED ARTICLES

"The Role of Education in the Economic Transformation of the State of St. Kitts-Nevis-Anguilla, 1950–1969, *Caribbean Studies*, vol. 14, no. 4, 1975, pp 89–107

"Factors Constraining Growth of Microstate Economies" in *Proceedings of the Conference on Environmental Management and Economic Growth in the Smaller Caribbean Islands*, William S. Beller, (Ed.) Department of State Publications 8996, November, 1979, pp 31–41

"Spatial Diffusion of Nursing Services from the Commonwealth Caribbean to Britain," in *Source Book on the New Immigration* Roy Simon, Bryce-Laporte, Editor, Transaction Books, New Jersey, 1980, pp 109–126

"Nieo: An Exercise According to the Sisyphean Fable," *Transition*, Issue 8, 1983, pp 37–54

"Subsidies, Tax Reliefs and Public Policy: The Development Aspects," in *Subsidies, Tax Reliefs and Prices*, Karl Hauser, Editor, Editions Cujas, France, 1977, pp 223–234

"Rational Expectations, Causality and Integrative Fiscal and Monetary Policy in the Caribbean, "*Social and Economic Studies*, Jamaica, Vol. 34, No. 4 1985, pp 111-138

OTHER INFORMATION

Assistant Chief Examiner, Caribbean Examinations Council, Principles of Business 1983 — Present

Member of the Board of Trustees of the University of the Virgin Islands, 1989-1990

Two-Time Chairman of the Faculty (Senate) of the University, 1987-88 and 1988-89

Chairman of the Presidential Search Committee of the University of the Virgin Islands, 1990

Human Resources in the Caribbean
FUAT M. ANDIC

It is with immense pleasure and satisfaction that I am addressing you tonight as the President of the Association of Caribbean Studies (sic), an honor which was bestowed upon me a year ago. This, for me, was the single greatest honor of my entire professional life. I thank my colleagues and friends for their confidence in me.

It is also an immense pleasure to see so many distinguished scholars and guests gathered around the theme of "Human Values and Human Resources in the Caribbean" in celebrating the tenth anniversary of our association.

Ever since its inception, the association has explored several aspects of the problematic of the Caribbean. This year we bend over the problems of human values and human resources. It would be far fetched for me to talk to you about human values after so eminent a scholar like Rex Nettleford. His magnificent speech Wednesday night leaves all of us speechless . . . What I wish to do tonight, as the last function of the out-going president, is to share with you some of my thoughts on human resources.

Before doing so, I cannot help but reminisce for a few minutes about the history of our association and share with you some of the values it holds in high esteem: values that bind its members together; values that have nourished and strengthened it during this past decade.

It was ten years ago here in San Juan that a handful of scholars, with professional interest in the study of the Caribbean, gathered together to celebrate the first conference of our association. They were but a handful of university professors and public servants, and they gave birth to the association. Like most births, it was not without pains. Divisive tendencies manifested their presence during that first conference, whatever the reasons might have been. In fact, there was an attempt to set up a counter conference, and I might add without success. Wild accusations were made, meetings were interrupted, and frictions arose among lifelong friends.

But, that is all history now. Many who attempted to organize the counter-conference then are among us today, as distinguished scholars, respected and listened to. Many of you may now know the history of the association as few of us here do. We were thirty then, we are over five hundred today.

It is not without recompense to ask ourselves what made us grow, what made us a respected professional organization. In my mind the answer is rather simple. The commitment to values of scholarship; tolerance; and mutual respect. The political views of the membership extend over every possible stand in the spectrum. That is a most welcome characteristic of the association. We embrace every liberal arts discipline, because we learn from each other. We do not care where our members were born, but we do care how seriously we study the Caribbean. We do not care what color our skin is, but we do care how dedicated we are. We do not attach importance to gender, but we do attach importance to what our scholarly aim is. We have no quotas—nor shall we ever have one—for minorities, based on skin color (white, black, yellow, or red), or sex, or religion, or place of birth. We do have, and we shall continue to have one single quota: those who wish to study any aspect of the Caribbean society objectively and those who wish to learn about the Caribbean society earnestly are in; those who do not are out. We have adhered and we will continue to adhere to this single value. We did in the past, and we came to be what we are today. And today is the end of the beginning.

Allow me now to turn to the problems of human resources in the Caribbean. Many of you have heard or discussed quite a number of papers on this particular aspect, or presented one. If I were to summarize most of the findings in one sentence, I would say that our basic wealth in the Caribbean is human resources. But, given the natural resource configuration of the Caribbean, we are apt to wonder how far we can go, given our human resources. We sometimes despair that we are overcrowded. We incline to think that historical circumstances have placed on us the unbearable burden of having been colonies for half a milenium. We consider the existing level of poverty to be an insurmountable constraint for our development. But then we should ask ourselves: What must we do?

The question of what we should do for our economic and social development forces us to seek solutions to the limitations I just mentioned. Let us look at them one by one.

First, the question of overpopulation. Ever since the publication of Malthus's Treatise in 1798, we have been, in a way, brainwashed. Geometrically growing population and arithmetically increasing food supply have mesmerized us. As a result, we tend to think that there is a positive correlation between poverty and population density. Yet, nothing can be further from the truth. Two examples from third world countries illustrate my point: Jamaica to Ethiopia. Thirty Ethiopians per square kilometer obviously compare very favorably with Jamaica's density ratio of two hundred. However, GNP per capita is $200 in Ethiopia while it is $1,500 in Jamaica. The population density in Honduras is 36; in the Dominican Republic it is 116. Yet per capita GDP in Honduras is $600, while in the Dominican Republic it reaches $1,400.

One could say that such a comparison is irrelevant; for what matters, it can be argued, is the size of arable land, since deserts and mountains have little economic significance. This objection is also far from reality. The arable land density in Singapore is about one-fourth that of the Dominican Republic, but per capita income is five times greater in Singapore. Hong Kong has practically no arable land, but its per capita income reaches the $5,000 mark. El Salvador has arable land galore with a per capita income of $700.

Then the argument shifts once again. What counts, it is now argued, is the resource endowment. We then lament that the Caribbean has no natural resources, hence little chance for development. But Japan has practically no known natural resources and Mexico too many. If the natural resources were the determinant factors, Mexico's per capita income should have been $11,000 and Japan's $2,300, and not the other way around.

If, as is demonstrated by the examples I have given so far, the level of development bears little relationship to differences in natural resources or arable land or any other predetermined geographical conditions, what then would make the Caribbean develop? Before we begin to search for the relevant answers, we must tackle other myths.

Another explanation for underdevelopment is found in the legacy of colonialism. Colonialism, we are frequently told, has prevented the development of the third world because external forces have had a vested interest in keeping it underdeveloped. Even if the premise were to be taken at its face value, I still would go along with the old Chinese proverb which says:

> "He who blames only the past for the present ills, has no future."

It is high time that the Caribbean understood its past, but also looked ahead into its future. We cannot change the past, but we can, and must, shape the future.

How do we shape our future? The question is easier stated than answered, and the answer is easier phrased than implemented. For years, nay, for decades we placed the emphasis on investment. Most economists believed that if investment were increased in an underdeveloped country, the vicious circle would be broken, the economy would grow at a much faster rate, and *presto*, we would be out of the woods of underdevelopment. We became investment fetishists. Although it was basically quite correct to assume that investment was a missing ingredient, miscalculations led us to uneconomic steelmills, overcapacity harbors, empty national airlines, highways from nowhere to nowhere which became the norm rather than the exception and wasted valuable real resources and burdened the economies with inflation, balance of payments difficulties, and other ills that followed from the wrong implementation of a good idea.

Why did we fail? We failed because we had not gone beyond Smith, Ricardo and Marx. We conceived the three factors of as three homogeneous entities. We had land which we assumed homogeneous entities. We had labor which we also assumed homogeneous; we did not have capital and we argued it was the missing element. Thirty or forty years ago we were still classical economists a la Smith or a la Marx.

I do not wish to be misconstrued. I am not saying that investment was not necessary for development. It certainly was and is. Our mistake stemmed from treating physical investment as the primary and decisive determinant of economic performance and from our long-time neglect or another type of investment: investment in labor or, as we refer to it, "human capital formation." It also stemmed from our singling out one factor alone, among many, as the determinant of growth rather than paying attention to the combined role of many.

Let me briefly mention past errors along this vein. As every economist knows, for the physiocrats the engine of economic growth was agriculture; for the classical economists it was the free market; for protectionists and the Marxists it was the capital; for Schumpeter it was the creative destruction; for Stalinists it was industrialization; and for structuralists it was import substitution. All embodied the three homogeneous factors of land, labor, and capital. To this scenario the geographers added their contribution, namely natural endowment, and political scientists added theirs of political stability.

None of these models in the long run gave an acceptable explanation of the growth process. We are now beginning to understand that each was lacking a number of intangibles. Physical factors alone cannot determine our growth. We have to incorporate into them a series of intangible factors, such as the quality and vision of the leadership, new market opportunities, and the change in the mentality from a pre-industrial to an industrial outlook, and the existence and realiability of skilled workers. In other words, human capital formation, or heterogeneity of labor. Emergence from poverty requires changes in attitudes of mores adverse to material improvement, readiness to produce for the market, and the pursuit of appropriate government policies.

In our Caribbean we do not have all the elements that generate growth. We do not have vast coal or iron ore mines. We do not have oil wells overflowing. But we do have, by and large, a better outlook towards the development process than many traditional societies. We have had and will continue to have political leadership with vision. Luis Munoz Marin, Norman Manley, Eric Williams are but three examples of such leadership. But most important of all, we do have a labor force that can be our biggest and best asset.

We must, however, learn to look upon this labor force as a heterogeneous factor. This required the pursuit of appropriate government policies in formulating and implementing manpower development strategies to train and upgrade human resources paying special attention to skills required to absorb and transform know-how into process design, development, commercialization and adaptation to changing circumstances. It also required sincere efforts to help the emergence of broadly based local entrepreneurship which is the human input into innovation and is not a homogeneous function. Rather it becomes more complex and more technical as economic development proceeds and as management control evolves from simple into highly sophisticated situations.

I should like to quote from the July 1984 *Nassau Understanding*, a declaration signed by the heads of government of the Caribbean community. This *Understanding* suggests, and I quote:

> ". . . programs (should) include management training, assistance with identifying sources of technology and venture capital as well as access to the range of commercial and financial services essential for business development . . . There are unique opportunities to be grasped by local entrepreneurs . . . In furtherance of the objective to involve the population more closely in development . . . Governments (should) agree to pay major attention to strengthening the educational system *at all levels* offering opportunities for the acquisition of skills that will directly contribute to the modernization and development of the economy."

We should heed the suggestion of the *Nassau Understanding* in differentiating and dehomogenising our labor force; we must create local entrepreneurs; local skilled workers; technicians; engineers, so that in the input-mix labor becomes an important component. Education represents an investment in the only reliable source of our small countries. Let us, therefore, invest in *our people*.

BRIEF BIOGRAPHY

NAME Fuat M. Andic

DATE OF BIRTH January 31 1927

ACADEMIC DEGREES Ph.D. University of Edinburgh, 1961

M.A. University of Michigan, 1956

B.A. University of Istanbul, 1949

ACADEMIC AFFILIATION Professor of Economics, University of Puerto Rico

BOOKS *What Price Equity: A Macroeconomic Analysis of the Economy of Costa Rica* University of Puerto Rico, 1983

Readings in Caribbean Public Sector Economics (Co-edited with S. B. Jones-Hendrickson) ISER, 1981

Politics and Economics in the Caribbean Edited with T. Mathews, University of Puerto Rico, 1971

A Theory of Integration among Developing Countries, (with S. Andic and D. Dosser), London: Allen & Unwin, 1971

Government Finance and Planned Development (with S. Andic), University of Puerto Rico 1968

SELECTED ARTICLES

"Costa Rica: A Macroeconomic Evaluation of Public Policy," prepared for USAID/PPC/E/S, June 1982

"Tax Harmonization among Developing Countries" Report Submitted to Inter-American Development Bank, September 1982

"An Economic Analysis of Residential Construction in Puerto Rico," February, 1978

"An Economic Analysis of the Carbonated Beverage Industry in Puerto Rico," June 1977

"National Income of Puerto Rico, 1920-1929," *Caribbean Studies* Vol. 2, No. 1, 1962

"Problems of Labor Legislation in Turkey," *Middle Eastern Affairs*, Vol. 3, No. 11, 1957

OTHER INFORMATION

Independent Consultant with International Organizations (UNDP, IMF, UNIDO, USAID, ETC) 1976-1982

Counsellor, Governor's Council on Labor and Social Policy, Government of Puerto Rico (Ad Honorem) 1977-present

Chief Economic Advisor, Tax Reform Commission, Government of Puerto Rico 1973-1975

Economic Aspects of the Relationship Between State and People in the Caribbean

COMPTON BOURNE

Rare (perhaps non-existent) is the Caribbean country in which relationships between the State as the embodiment of governmental power, obligations and rights and the People are felicitous. Furthermore, the recent course of political events in several countries on both the left and the right of the ideological spectrum has focussed attention very sharply on the normative question of what should be the central tendencies in that relationship.

Caribbean people have not been silent on the normative issue; nor can it be said that the intelligentsia has been reluctant to declare its several positions. However, the issue is of such fundamental importance that it warrants considerably more sustained analytical attention than Caribbean scholars have been inclined to devote. In the totality of such analyses, it would be necessary to proceed not only axiomatically in terms of principles of political and social theory, but also to distil from the past and present realities of State-People relationship.

This address deals with only one of the many facets of the relationship. It focusses on a few economic aspects, even though the interaction of politics and economics cannot be denied. Indeed, it begins with political matters.

POLITICAL PROFILES OF STATE-PEOPLE RELATIONSHIP

The relationship between State and People in the Caribbean cannot be uniformly categorised. On the basis of political characteristics, Carl Stone, in his Power in the Caribbean Basin, identifies three main types of political regimes: democratic-pluralist, authoritarian, and populist-statist. The assignment of a particular regime to one of other category depends upon its performance relative to four core attributes of a political system, namely, mass political participation, political rights, interests representation, and ideology.

It is useful to set out Stone's schema before classifying contemporary Caribbean regimes. Democratic pluralist regimes are typified by the widespread participation of the people in selection of the political elite and in the design and monitoring of government policies, by strong civil rights and moderate social rights, and by voluntaristic and extensive autonomous group representation. In the democratic-pluralist State, economic policies are centrist and reformist; dissent is encouraged. The authoritarian State prohibits mass political participation (except through fictional Workers' Parties and command performances at mass rallies). Civil rights are suppressed and legal control and order emphasized. Economic policies are conservative and interest group representation highly structured. Populist-Statist regimes restrict people participation in policy formulation while requiring it for policy implementation. "Individual political rights are suppressed in the interests of party discipline. Emphasis is placed instead on social and economic rights". (Stone 1985, p. 15). The political party serves as the organ for interest representation and as a mechanism for social unity. Economic policies are intended to be transformative.

There are likely to be objections to any political classification of Caribbean States, but this section of the address would be incomplete without an updating and modification of Stone's categorization. Among the authoritarian regimes may be listed Guatemala, Honduras, Haiti, Surinam, and possibly Panama. The populist-statist group includes Nicaragua, Cuba, and Guyana. All others are in the democratic-pluralist category: the remaining ten Commonwealth Caribbean States, three Hispanic States (Venezuela, Republica Dominicana, and Costa Rica), and the Netherland Antilles. The British dependencies, the French Antilles, Puerto Rico, and the U.S. Virgin Islands are Caribbean extensions of non-Caribbean States.

Clearly, the democratic-pluralist model is the numerically predominant type. Attention is therefore directed mainly to economic aspects of State-People relationship within this model.

ECONOMIC ASPECTS OF DEMOCRATIC-PLURALIST SYSTEMS

The many strands to the economic role of the State in democratic-pluralist systems enforce some selectivity in this address. However, an attempt is made to deal with two broad aspects of State-People economic relationship in a manner that analytically integrates much of the minutae of actual policies and interactions.

ECONOMIC PATRON

The first concerns the role of the State as 'patron' or even "padrone". One distinct feature of State economic policy in democratic-pluralist Caribbean regimes is the policy objective of substantial improvements in the material welfare of the people. (Whether one regards this objective as proximate or ultimate depends very much on the degree of one's political cynicism). The pursuit of this objective is not evenhanded. The grossly unequal distribution of purchasing power within these communities has its corollary in redistributive expenditures, income transfers, and employment policies. It cannot even be said that policies have been consistent at any moment in time or sustained through the years for, as stated later, this has not been so. However, what is being emphasized now is the central tendency, the essential nature of this class of policies. As 'patron', the State accepts the responsibility for raising levels of living with the society.

This role model is the outcome of two not necessarily contradictory elements. One is the welfarist principle. The colonial origins of modern day Caribbean States has acutely sensitized political directorates to the material aspirations of Caribbean peoples and to their sense of relative deprivation within world society. A major shift in intellectual understanding of the meaning of development reinforces the welfarist principle. The new view in economic development sees man as the subject of development so that economic development is measured by the degree to which it provides for the material and creative advancement of the society. Basic needs and general human progress become central to economic policy. The notion is, of course, not new, for what else could the influential 16th century English theologian, Richard Hooker, have meant when he wrote in his "Of the Laws of Ecclesiatical Polity" that men unite themselves in political societies to provide "a life fit for the dignity of man".

The welfarist principle admits of a functional rationalization in strict economic terms. As we have been told by Nobel Laureate Theodore Schultz (1961), people are also human capital. If education is an investment in human capital, then food, shelter and medical care are essential capital maintenance expenditures.

In essence, we may simply quote from Gunnar Myrdal's Asian Drama (1968):

"Levels of living are of course important in themselves. . . . But in addition, a rise in the levels of living has an instrumental value. By the circular causation attending changes in social condition, a rise in levels of living is likely to improve almost all other conditions, in particular labour input and efficiency and thus productivity, but also attitudes and institutions."

The other element in the 'patron' role of the State is the pursuit and retention of political power. This is the element granted primacy by political analysts. To the poor, especially, bread in exchange for ballots may not be an entirely unattractive proposition. Patronage, of course, is not identical to the concept of patron utilised here. The latter is much broader and all-embracing, not being limited (as patronage is) to essentially interpersonal economic relationships.

Furthermore, there is some doubt about the efficacy of patronage in electoral competition. In an excellent study entitled Class, State and Democracy in Jamaica, Carl Stone (1986, pg. 61) concludes that "The generous handouts of political patronage are, . . . never adequate to influence the national vote to significantly enhance a party's chances of re-election. It is the main thrust of social and economic policies and the benefits they seem to be generating within the society as a whole that is crucial to maintaining a party's credibility".

The manifestations of the 'patron' role of the State are myriad: selective employment programmes, commodity pricing policies, income redistribution, subsidies and transfers. It is impossible to discuss all of these instruments, mechanisms and policies in detail, or indeed, to discuss any particular one at this time. This address is confined to a few evaluative comments.

The State has not been notably successful in its welfare policies; quite the contrary in several instances. Selective employment programmes have provided only partial and temporary alleviation of chronic unemployment, income inequality and poverty persists, and large percentages of the relevant age cohorts have no access to secondary and tertiary education. This is not to deny the social validity of sometimes heroic efforts or the fact of some success, but to emphasize the limited nature of the gains from these types of operations.

It is instructive to consider the reasons for the limited success of welfarist economic policies. One reason may be generally described as policy design failures. These include inappropriate choice of policy instruments. With some instruments, the channel of influence is too indirect for certainty, the policy intent is more easily evaded or distorted, and benefits appropriated by persons other than the intended beneficiaries. Thus, for example, producer subsidies rather than direct consumer subsidies to achieve nutrition targets, experience problems of erosion by inflation, are irrelevant insofar as intended beneficiaries do not have the income base for entering the commodity market, and are prone to misappropriation by either wage labour or capital.

Other types of policy design failures are inconsistencies within the entire framework of State economic policy, and insufficient appreciation of financial constraints. Perhaps, a brief word on these two types is in order. Partly because of fragmentation of policy decision and implementation at governmental level and partly because of the multiplicity of goals and constituents, policy inconsistencies are frequent. The consequences of policy inconsistencies are mutual negation, confusion within the bureaucracy and society, and high delivery costs. The financial constraint is a major problem for welfarist governments in the Caribbean. Not only is fiscal capacity and performance typically weak in both static and dynamic contexts, but financial flows to the public sector are highly unstable as a consequence of the structures of the domestic economy and the international economy and the relationship between them. Unexpected decreases in resource flows have forced reversals in welfare policies at a pace not independent of "distress" borrowing from the multilateral financial institutions.

The presence of intervening institutional variables must be a cardinal element in the explanation of the relative failure of welfarist policies in Caribbean democratic-pluralist systems. Much has been written by political scientists on the role of lobbies and bureaucrats in the formulation and transmission of economic policies, stressing the idea that power and influence are harnessed in the economic service of particular interest groups. Economists have not added much, contributing only the trite observation that bureaucrats have their own independent preference functions and that they may seek to maximise these instead of the State's social preference function.

ECONOMIC REGULATION

The second broad aspect of State-People economic relationship discussed in this address is economic regulation. As

Richard Posner (1974) notes: "Properly defined, the term refers to taxes and subsidies of all sorts, as well as explicit legislative and administrative controls over rates, entry, and other facets of economic activity." A curious feature of Caribbean societies is the conjuncture of a proliferation of economic regulations and their avoidance or evasion by individuals and businesses. Many Caribbean intellectuals are themselves regulatory-minded, whether they are ideologically "right" or "left".

Several reasons have been proffered for regulatory action. The most universal is the occurrence of market failure. By "market failure", economists mean not the absence of profits or anything like that, but rather the presence of structural impediments to the achievement of a situation of pure competition and the associated unattainability of the criteria for socially efficient allocation, production and pricing. Natural and created monopolies, positive and negative externalities, and public goods are critical elements in the theory of market failure. Administrative regulations, taxes and subsidies, are the main State responses. But the logic of market failure can also lead to direct production and supply by the State, that is to State ownership and control of the means of production. While not strictly a regulatory response, State production is conveniently clustered with economic regulations for the purpose of this address. In the instance of market failure, economic regulation is perceived or at least rationalized in terms of the public interest.

Economic crises constitute another basis for economic regulation. These crises are typically in the macroeconomic system—price inflation, ever widening balance of payments deficits and foreign exchange insufficiency, and sharp contractions in employment. But the crises are occasionally microeconomic or industry specific. They become of general national concern only because of the strategic importance of the industry or enterprise in the overall socio-economic milieu. Whether micro or macro in nature, economic crises generate pressures or demands for immediate ameliorative or corrective action. In financially weak States, the response is frequently regulatory: foreign exchange restrictions, price controls, labour market intervention, and public sector takeovers. In these circumstances, regulations are a form of crisis management characteristically short-term in intent, but as experience has shown, with a tendency to outlive their original justification.

Economic regulations are not motivated purely by the public interest. Particular interest groups may stand to gain from specific regulatory actions and may be willing to expend economic resources in persuading the State that their private interests converge with the public interest. Witness, for instance, the efforts of the textile lobby in Trinidad and Tobago and in the USA. This dimension of economic regulation has been emphasized by scholars such as George Stigler (1971), Richard Posner (1974), and Sam Peltzman (1976).

Regulations are manifestations of power, but this exercise of power is neither certain or unmitigated. Policy intentions can be frustrated, distorted and perverted during the complex interplay of political and economic forces. Lester Salamon and John Siegfried (1977) state one problem very well:

". . . the (democratic pluralist) political system offers relatively easy access by citizens to the central policymaking process on a regular basis. While this relative permeability raises the possibility of broad public control of governmental policy à la pure democratic theory, however, it also raises the paradoxical possibility of translating disproportionate economic power into disproportionate political influence in a way that can frustrate broad public control."

Salamon and Siegfried stress the disproportionate influence of large firms as a result of the maldistribution of incentives for political action and the unequal distribution of "politically relevant resources" such as money, expertise and access to government officials. Gunnar Myrdal identifies pervasive bureaucratic corruption in what he terms the "soft State". In the soft State, we are reminded, there is a weak sense of loyalty to organised society. Corruption prevails. To paraphrase the Trinidadian calypsonian Lord Kitchener, everyone is corrupt; only those caught are guilty. Neoclassical economists exemplified by Stigler and Peltzman explain the particular forms of regulatory policies and their outcomes in terms of differential costs and benefits to demanders and suppliers of regulatory policies in a utility maximisation framework. The economic approach is quite consistent with the seemingly sociological theory of corruption. It can be argued, as by Edward Banfield (1975), that regulations, particularly when they confer monopoly powers on governmental organisations, create strong economic incentives for corruption.

Perhaps, Edward Kane's (1977, 1981) "regulatory dialectics" best describes the process or fate of regulations in democratic pluralist societies. In the regulatory dialectics there are two opposing forces (the political side and the economic side) each reacting in lagged response to actions taken by the other. To Kane, the flow of events in a regulated market is a three-stage process of regulation, avoidance, and re-regulation. Differences in the structure of incentives to bureaucrats and regulatees explain why the regulatory and re-regulatory response is generally less swift than the avoidance response.

THE DEVELOPMENT IMPERATIVE AND THE LURE OF AUTHORITARIANISM

Democratic-pluralist States in the Caribbean are perpetually under threat from persons partial to State-populist and authoritarian political ideologies. The intellectual bases of the lure of these forms of political regimes are quasi-historical, political and economic. The rather naive quasi-historical argument adduces the rapid economic growth of the Eastern European countries under totalitarian social systems and the development contrasts between the long established democratic pluralist countries of Western Europe and North America and the nascent political nations of the Third World. In these quasi-historical models, political democracy is a luxury to be traded or surrendered in exchange for rapid material progress.

The political factors are more subtle, seductive and extensive. Myrdal (1968) thinks that corruption paves the way for authoritarian regimes "whose disclosure of corrupt practices in the preceding government and whose punitive actions against offenders provide the basis for its acceptance by the articulate strata of the population". Carl Stone, in his Jamaican work (1986, pp; 53–54), attributes the appeal of authoritarianism in post-colonial societies to the psychological needs of party rank and file for strong authority figures. The Westminister model of parliamentary democracy itself is criticised on the grounds that it is divisive, while what is required for development is social unity. To Michael Best (1971), "the ideology of individualism . . . is for the underclass . . . an ideology of frustration and impotence". Frederick Nunes (1976) declares bluntly:

> "It is our view that a neutral bureaucracy is ill-suited to the needs of poor developing countries and that the two-party

political system divides societies into warring camps instead of unifying communities and building nations. The axiom which follows from these views is that a politicized bureaucracy in a one-party state may more effectively accomplish the modernization process.'

Evidently, economic notions permeate the political considerations just listed. At bottom is the belief or the conclusion that democratic pluralism is inconsistent with rapid economic development and that less democratic forms may be prerequisites or conjoints of material advancement. It is attenuated by the serious difficulties and correlated cynicism associated with welfarist and regulatory policies of the democratic-pluralist State. The development imperative becomes a powerful lure to statism and authoritarianism.

With lures, things are not what they seem. The promise is belied by the reality. In the field of economic development, there is no empirical validity to the association claimed between type of political regime and societal welfare. International cross-section data reveal no correlation between the three types of political regimes and national economic performance and quality of life indicators. In the light of the experiences of many authoritarian regimes in the 20th century, those who succumb to the lure may well find themselves exchanging the certainty of at least minimum human rights for the illusion of economic gain.

REFERENCES

Banfield, Edward C (1975) "Corruption as a Feature of Governmental Organisation," *Journal of Law and Economics* 18, 3: 587–605
Best, Michael, H (1971) "Uneven Development and Dependent Market Economies," *American Economic Review* (May) 136–41
Kane, Edward J. (1981) "Accelerating Inflation, Technological

Innovation and the Decreasing Effectiveness of Banking Regulation". *Journal of Finance* 36: 355-367

Kane, Edward J (1977) "Good Intentions and Unintended Evil: The Case Against Selective Credit Control". *Journal of Money, Credit and Banking*, 9: 55-69

Lord Kitchener (1983) "Soca Corruption" from the album, *Simply Wonderful*.

Myrdal, Gunnar (1968) *Asian Drama: An Inquiry into the Poverty of Nations*, Middlesex, England: Penguin Books.

Nunes, F. E. (1976) "The Nonsense of Neutrality". *Social and Economic Studies* 25, 4 (December) 347-66.

Peltzman, Sam (1976) "Towards a More General Theory of Regulation". *Journal of Law and Economics* 19, 2: 211-240

Posner, Richard A. (1974) "Theories of Economic Regulation", *Bell Journal of Economics and Management Science* 2, 5: 335-358.

Salaman, Lester M. & Siegfried, John J. "Economic Power and Political Influence The Impact of Industry Structure on Public Policy". *American Political Science Review* 71, 3: 1026-1043

Stigler, George J. (1971) "The Theory of Economic Regulation" *Bell Journal of Economics and Management Science* 2: 3-21.

Stone, Carl (1985) *Power in the Caribbean Basin: A Comparative Study of Political Economy* Philadelphia: Institute for the Study of Human Issues.

Stone, Carl (1986) *Class, State and Democracy in Jamaica* New York: Praeger Publishers.

BRIEF BIOGRAPHY

NAME   Compton Bourne

DATE OF   October 7 1943
BIRTH

ACADEMIC DEGREES	Ph.D. University of the West Indies Jamaica, 1975
	M.S. University of Birmingham England, 1968 (Economics)
	B.Sc Woolwich Polytechnic, London England, Studied for University of Longon 1967 (Economics)
ACADEMIC AFFILIATIONS	Pro-Vice Chancellor for Planning and Vice-Principle, UWI, St. Augustine Trinidad
	Chairman, Department of Economics University of the West Indies St. Augustine Campus, 1987 – Present
	Dean, Faculty of Social Sciences, The University of the West Indies, St. Augustine Campus.
	Chairman, Faculty of Social Sciences Sub-Committee of Board for Higher Degrees, University of the West Indies
BOOKS	*Caribbean Development to the Year 2000* Commonwealth Secretariat, London, 1988
	Money and Finance in Trinidad and Tobago (Co-Authored with Ramesh Ramsaran), Kingston, Jamaica: *Institute of Social and Economic Research*, April 1989
	Editor, Special Issue of *Social and Economic Studies* Vol. 34, No. 4 December, 1985 (Essays in Memory of Adlith Browne), 218 pages
	Editor, *Rural Financial Markets in*

Jamaica: (Special Issue of Social and Economic Studies, Vol. 32, No. 1, 1983), 170 pages

Joint Author (Colin C. Weir, E. Le Franc, and F. E. Nunes), *Small Farming in the Less Developed Countries of the Commonwealth Caribbean*, (Barbados, Caribbean Development Bank, 1980), 355 pages

SELECTED ARTICLES

"Financial Deepening, Domestic Resource Mobilization and Economic Growth in Jamaica, 1955–1982" in Antonio Jorge and Jorge Salazar-Carillo (Eds.) *Foreign Investment, Debt, and Economic Growth in latin America* New York: Macmillan Press, 1988

"Economic Disequilibria and Rural Financial Market Performance in the Commonwealth Caribbean", *Proceedings, West Indian Agricultural Economics Conference*, 1987

"Financial Implications of the Energy Crisis for Dependent Under-Developed Economies", *Micro-State Studies*, 3, 1982, (Co-Authored with W. H. Persaud)

"Notes on Financial Changes in Trinidad Tobago: 1966–1978", *Social and Economic Studies* 31, 4, 1982: 171–191.

"External Debt and Economic Growth in the Commonwealth Caribbean", pp. 109–112 in Antonio Jorge, Jorge Salazar-Carillo and Rene Higonnett (Eds.), *Foreign Debt and Latin American*

Economic Development, (Pergamon Press, 1982)

"Government Foreign Borrowing and Economic Growth: The Case of Jamaica" *Social and Economic Studies*, 30, 4, 1981 53-74.

OTHER INFORMATION

Coordinator, Caribbean Regional Programme of Monetary Studies (Research)

Vice-President, Institute of Social and Economic Research in the Caribbean Basic (Iescaribe), 1985

Vice-President, Caribbean Agro-Economic Society, 1982-1986

SECTION III

Challenges Of Leadership
ALMA H. YOUNG

> Life is one big road with lots of signs
> so when your riding thru the ruts
> Don't complicate your mind
> Flee from hate, mischief and jealousy
> Don't bury your thoughts
> Put your vision to reality
>
> *—Bob Marley & The Wailers (1979)*
> *from the song "Wake Up and Live"*

As we participate in the XII International Congress in Belize, it is appropriate that we reflect on the strengths of CSA and its role in the field of Caribbean Studies. First, our membership continues to grow, with a significant number of new members having joined in the last several months. Second, our membership continues to be diverse, with individuals from throughout the Caribbean, the United States, Europe and now Central America as a result of the annual meeting being held in Belize this year. Third, membership is still barred to institutions, to ensure that CSA is not captive to any powerful blocs or interests. Fourth, the Council, which is now more representative of the membership in terms of nationality and gender, is beginning to be structured into committees, which means that more can be accomplished in a timely manner. The Council has been an active resource all year long. Fifth, we now have the authority to speak out on public policy issues affecting the Caribbean. With this authority we can use the expertise of our members to help shape public policies in the area. Finally, as the field of Caribbean Studies has become more widely accepted as a valid area of inquiry, CSA has become known as the premier interdisciplinary organization of Caribbeanists. The changes we have talked about taking place in CSA are all changes that have made the organization more participatory and more democratic. And democracy is what I want to talk about, that old-fashioned concept that is frequently discussed today but so often maligned and misused. When I was an undergraduate studying government in the late '60s democracy was a major topic of inquiry; by the time I went to graduate school in the '70s democracy somehow seemed suspect and discussion centered around other political topics. Today democracy is back at center stage: in the U.S. the "preservation of democracy" is a hallmark of our foreign policy; countless organizations have been established, some overtly and others covertly, to support democracy: these include the National Endowment for Democracy, established by Congress in 1983; the National Endowment for the Preservation of Liberty, established by rogue elements in the National Security Advisor's office; the Inter-American Center for Educational Assistance and Promotion of Liberty.

In the Caribbean, especially the English-speaking Caribbean, discussion centers around the possible loss of democracy, as governments become more authoritarian and the military becomes a more significant part of the political process. One of the main concerns facing the Caribbean is how to keep the military from leaving the barracks? In Central America, and throughout Latin America, there is much discussion about the "redemocratization process," or the withdrawal of the military from positions of government and the subsequent installation of democratically elected civilians.

As the military returns to the barracks, the question is to what extent does the political order really become democratic?

Unfortunately the "democracy" which has become fashionable lately is often a shallow conception of the real term and the elements chosen to characterize democracy serve the self-interests and specific purposes of the groups advocating it. Latin America's efforts to create a democratic order has been called "the most stunning and moving political fact of recent years." The U.S. points with pride to the democratic transition taking place from the Dominican Republic and Grenada to El Salvador and Guatemala. Yet we know that this redemocratization is limited in scope, with the military still playing a controlling role in the political process.

We know that the military regime attempts to control the progression of "redemocratization" by favoring civilian partners who emphasize legal-political changes over socioeconomic structural transformations. These favored civilian partners focus on changing institutions of government and not the state. The military also encourages "incremental changes"—the process of change is staggered in discrete stages, thus allowing for the dispersion of the opposition. Therefore, the process enables the military and its favored partners to bargain and trade off changes for continuities.

In order to segment the opposition the military establishes "parameters" as to who is eligible to participate and who is excluded. The purpose is to divide "moderates" from "radicals", so that the latter can be marginalized and reduced to a secondary force. Finally we must remember that the military returns to the barracks as a way of pre-emptying anticipated opposition. The process of redemocratization reflects the military's difficulty in ruling, its growing sense of political isolation, its realization that the process of conflict could escalate to a point where the situation could completely escape from their control and present for them totally unacceptable alternatives. Therefore, the redemocratization process can be seen as a pre-emptive strike by the military in the face of the deepening economic crisis and growing social movements with their increasing struggle to create political space. The concern of the military is to shift the problem from the street to the negotiating table where it can be more easily handled . . . The "revolution" is coopted and contained. The decision to withdraw to the barracks is much more a decision to avoid the totally unattractive choices inherent in a deepening polarization than a conversion to democratic politics.

Yet, the United States continues to praise the shift towards democratic regimes that they see as evident throughout the Caribbean Basin. Democracy is viewed in the limited sense of electoral choice; yet we know how electoral choice can be manipulated and emasculated. Beyond that, the United States still holds to its historic definition of what constitutes a democratic ally: one who does not threaten United States national security, political or economically. In order to support what they perceive as the "remarkable trend towards democracy" taking place in the region, the Reagan Administration in its Fiscal Year 1988 request to Congress seeks two main kinds of assistance for the Caribbean. The administration is requesting $271.6 million in military assistance and $1.3 billion in economic assistance. Both the economic and military aid tend to draw the countries closer to the U.S. sphere of influence—to bind them to the United States. Beyond that, one might question the need for so much military aid at a time when the democratic process is supposed to be taking hold.

The large sums of military aid are in keeping with the essence of the Reagan Administration's Foreign Policy, which is to actually overthrow wherever possible, and not simply to contain, socialist governments in the region. The aid being poured into the region is an attempt at containment of socialist forces *and* an attempt to fight the socialists through a proxy war. In Nicaragua the U.S. goal is not direct intervention but covert warfare, a war of attrition, with economic destabilization being a major element. That policy has resulted in several years of zero economic growth in Nicaragua, where 40% of the budget is needed for military defense, and therefore essential social and economic programs have had to be cut back. The benefits of the revolution are slowly being decimated. The people suffer enormously—as the battle for "democracy vs socialism" is played out in international arenas. Of course Nicaragua is only one of the areas where the rollback of socialist or quasi-socialist regimes is being played out. We cannot forget Grenada, or Manley's Jamaica or Jagan's Guyana.

In the Commonwealth Caribbean we have long lived with the myth that the British bequeathed enduring democratic traditions and institutions to its former colonies. The masses have been manipulated, politicized, mobilized and demobilized to such an extent that the *form* of democracy has often been equated with the social and political *content* of democracy. But even the myth of democracy is being shattered as the authoritarian state becomes more commonplace. The development of the authoritarian state is reflected most clearly in the broadening of the scope of the military and security instruments of state power. Throughout the region the military and security apparatus is expanding through increased financial outlays for military purchases, training and technical assistance. Repression is on the increase, and governments are more and more relying on the use of violence by extralegal gangs and paramilitary units against the opposition. Security and legislative means are used to demobilize the working class in its struggle for just compensation. Electoral and legal processes are being manipulated to serve the objectives of the regime, most of which have lost genuine popular support and now rely on creating their own "mass" base to legitimize their unpopular rule.

Security forces are becoming increasingly politicized. The danger is that the military, coming to see itself as the savior or protector of their countries, will become major political bargainers in the region. Washington's interests would be served by such a development, for it would ensure a certain amount of stability, since the masses would be dissuaded from political and social action that might be useful in their struggle against exploitation and repression. Anticommunism and national security are the ideological weapons used by these regimes. Again, the interests of the Caribbean regimes coincide with those of Washington, where maintaining the national security of the hemisphere is viewed as critical, and the military aid pours in. For instance, security aid in the Eastern Caribbean has grown from approximately $4 million in 1980 to approximately $26 million in 1986.

The expansion and growing visibility of the military in Commonwealth Caribbean life is a direct result of the fact that the political and economical crisis facing the region has escalated to such a point that the traditional methods of cooptation and neutralization of the masses are no longer felt to be adequate. Repression is viewed as necessary, and with that comes the fact that the security apparatus begins to play a more prominent role in the political decision-making process. In the Caribbean, then, the military are beginning to come out of the barracks and the result is a further retarding of the people's "cry" for social change.

The struggle for social change that began with so much promise in the 1930s has never been allowed to fully develop. In the 1940s the revolution was headed off by universal adult suffrage and the formation of trade unions. In the 1950s the cry for change was muffled by the mass migration to the metropolis. In the 1960s we had the euphoria of political independence. In the 1970s there was the confusion of sloganeering and the importation of alien ideologies. Today the people voice their discontent through the ballot box—but the recent changing of the political guard throughout the (Commonwealth) Caribbean has brought only new faces into the halls of power, not new policies. Recently it has been asked whether general elections are not now the new opiate of the people.

When will the voice of the people, which began to be articulated in the 1930s, be fully heard? How do we bring about the political, social and economic transformation of the Caribbean so that our young men and women have meaningful work to fill their lives, our children have adequate food, our homes are decent, safe and secure, our work is justly compensated? As Pablo Neruda has asked, "when can we expect the justice of eating?"

We must create a situation where Caribbean peoples can be more active doers—capable of defining problems, identifying friends and foes, setting goals and opening up channels to a better future. In preparation for that, our excessive dependance on aid from the United States must stop. Barrow says that a "patronage mendicancy syndrome" now exists in the Caribbean. One of the key ways of weaning ourselves from over-reliance on United States aid is to develop a regional agenda, starting with the basics. Together we can develop a food sufficiency program, first outlined by Eric Williams. Only with food security can there be economic and political stability. Beyond that, food security is also a moral imperative, for the right to eat is as basic as the right to live.

Our regional institutions, such as the Caribbean Development Bank, need to be brought back to the center of regional planning, and strengthened. The multilateral approach to aid, where aid flows to and through our regional organizations, is more appropriate for the development of the Caribbean. The current bilateral policies not only lead to over-reliance on donor countries but encourage divisiveness in the region and competition for scarce resources.

Using its expertise the Caribbean needs to devise its own development schemes, not ones imported from abroad. With this approach the Caribbean will identify its own needs. We will reverse the crisis mentality that now grips us and instead face our own problems squarely—problems which center around how to produce for oneself.

As we grapple with the conference theme, THE CHALLENGE OF CHANGE: LEADERSHIP IN THE CARIBBEAN, let us work hard in our individual panels and in the plenaries to begin to develop an agenda for development in the Caribbean. An agenda needs to be fashioned that our leaders can use in their policy deliberations and programmatic decisions. As Bob Marley would say, let's make this meeting "a session and not a version." On the 100th anniversary of the birth of Marcus Garvey, let us remember the successes (and failures) of ordinary Caribbean men and women, banding together in self-help groups, in forging a vision of the Caribbean and the changes they wrought. Let us remember our leaders, from Bustamante to Bishop, from Marti to Munoz Marin, who took the people's vision and articulated an agenda for the region. The struggle for self-determination, equality and a better standard of living continues. Therefore, let us also remember the endemic problems that still plague the Caribbean, from poverty and unemployment to increased militarization and authoritarianism to capital flight and indebtedness. The '87 conference will provide the perspective needed for a rethinking of where we are and where we would like to be.

In the long run, however, the future of the Caribbean depends on the Caribbean people—on their having an instinct for history and survival and a determination to confront their adversaries. It means altering the relationship that the people now have with economic elites and with the government.

It means, in short, becoming more democratic, in both the legal-political *and* the socio-economic sense. It means no longer being lulled into complacency by the form of democracy without the substance of democracy. It means giving voice to the people's cry for the justice of eating and working and shelter.

It means therefore that there must be the free expression of consent *and* dissent; there must be freedom of speech, freedom of the press, freedom of assembly and association; there must be an independent judiciary; and there must be respect for human rights—the very foundation of democracy.

How do we achieve this? We must provide our children and ourselves with an education that is wide-ranging and that instills a sense of history. We can no longer afford an education that is censored, limited or parochial. The academic community must be committed to preparing our young people for the joys and responsibilities of living in a democratic society and preserving that democracy. We must provide students with enough history to be able to make their own value judgments about the form of government they would like to live under and the kinds of policies they would like to see pursued. We much teach the history of our own and other societies so that the student sees the values that are dominant in each and is in a position to judge them. The idea is to provide enough information so that the student understands that social contracts are not cost-free, but represent deliberate choices among conflicting values and that the price of paths followed can be high indeed, a matter of life and death, a matter of food or starvation.

During this time of economic and political crisis gripping the Caribbean we want our children to be able to discern the values and principles that are being pursued and those that are being sacrificed, often for immediate gratification. We want them to know that when someone says "everything is everything," that person is suspect. They must know and we must know that a just and humane society is worth the effort and that we will be content with nothing less.

REFERENCES

Chace, James (1984) *Endless War: How We Got Involved in Central America and What Can Be Done* New York: Vintage Books

Dixon, Marlene (1985) "Overview: Militarism and Foreign Policy—Reagan's Second Term, *Contemporary Marxism* No. 10, pp. i–xxiii. Dixon (1985) p. xix.

Petras, James (1987) "The Redemocratization Process." *Contemporary Marxism*, No. 14, pp. 1–15

Watson, Hilbourne A. (1986) "Imperialism, National Security, and State Power in the Commonwealth Caribbean: Issues and the Development of the Authoritarian State." In Alma H. Young and Dion E. Phillips, (Eds.) *Militarization in the Non-Hispanic Caribbean* Boulder, Colo. Lynne Rienner Publishers, pp. 17–41

BRIEF BIOGRAPHY

NAME   Alma H. Young

DATE OF BIRTH   February 11 1947

ACADEMIC DEGREES   Ph.D. Massachusetts Institute of Technology, 1978

M.S. Columbia University, 1970

A.B. Radcliffe College, 1969

ACADEMIC AFFILIATION	Professor, College of Urban and Public Affairs, University of New Orleans
BOOKS	Co-Editor (with Dion E. Phillips) and Contributor, *Militarization in the Non-Hispanic Caribbean* Boulder, Co: Lynne Reinner Publishers, 1986
SELECTED ARTICLES	Contributed Chapters on "Belize" for Volumes I–VII of *Latin America and Caribbean Contemporary Record* (1983–1989) New York: Holmes and Meier Publishers
	"Lessons for the Dutch-Speaking Caribbean from the Commonwealth Caribbean" (1990) Betty Sedoc-Dahlberg, Ed. *The Dutch Caribbean* New York: Gordon and Breach Publisher
	"Peace, Democracy and Security in the Caribbean" (forthcoming) J. Edward Greene and Jorge Rodriguez Bereff, Eds. *Peace and Development in the Caribbean.* MacMillan Press
	"The Impact of the 'Anglo-Guatemala Dispute' on the Internal Politics of Belize." (with Dennis H. Young) *Latin American Perspectives*, May, 1988 pp. 6–30
	"Black Ethnicity: A Theoretical Perspective" (1987) Alma H. Young, Ed. *The State of Black New Orleans.* A Publication of the Urban League of Greater New Orleans, pp. 59–79
	"U.S. Military Expansionism in the Eastern Caribbean: Guns Instead of Butter?" *Bulletin of Eastern Caribbean Affairs*, Vol.

11, No. 6 (January/February 1987), pp 19-22

OTHER INFORMATION

Special Assistant to the Mayor of New Orleans (Responsible for Office of Federal Programs and Special Projects) 1978-80

Chair, Board of Commissioners for the Port of New Orleans, 1989-90

Editor and Project Consultant, *The State of New Orleans*, 1985, 1986 1987 and 1988 (A Publication of the Urban League of Greater New Orleans).

Peace in the Caribbean: A Possible Utopia?

ANDRES SERBIN

I have not chosen tonight's theme haphazardly. Two reasons have justified my choice: In the first place, I think that in the current circumstances in which the region finds itself, there are more and more, and stronger, voices clamoring for the region to distance itself from the political vagaries imposed by the global confrontation and the interests of extraregional powers. And this clamor is more and more clearly pointing to the growing hope of converting the region into a zone of peace.

Secondly, my decision has been dictated by a moral debt to one who has promoted this aspiration within our association, trying to recruit the support of scholars of the region for a proposal that goes further than academic discussions. I wish, consequently, to begin by rendering a posthumous homage to Vera Rubin who motivated in me the first preoccupations with the theme of peace in the Caribbean. To Vera Rubin, we owe the proposal that the annual meeting of CSA would be held in Caracas in 1986 under the theme "Pacem in Maribus," an idea originally prompted by Eric Williams. The meeting was held in Caracas, but without Vera, and the central theme was changed. Only partially and belatedly can we repair this and it is for this reason that I wish to dedicate these words to her and her indefatigable commitment to the people of the region.

Much has been said about the true limits of the Caribbean as a region and about the characteristics that define it and make up its identity. Politicians, academics and poets have given abundant characterizations, from different perspectives and frequently, different prejudices and preconcepts. But the diverse definitions in vogue have not contributed to a conceptual clarification of the problem. Neither will I tonight. To comment on gestures and words, to dissect the most prominent traits, to clarify the ever changing limits imposed by the political history of the region, generally leads us to conclude only that the complex heterogeneity of the Caribbean is what gives it its identity and its difference in the world. It was not in vain that Sidney Mintz pointed out with respect to the Caribbean:

> "The despair of the classifiers, area studies programs, Kremlinologists in ill-fitting sombreros, North American race relations experts, ambulant East European comissars and the CIA, the Caribbean region goes its own way, richly researched but poorly understood" (Mintz, "The Caribbean Region," in *Daedalus*, Spring 1974).

So that while the Caribbean follows its own route, it does not make sense to begin these words with an anthology of definitions that threaten to convert this speech into one of the most boring in the history of CSA. Neither will I pretend, with the immodesty and narcissism that characterize our profession, to formulate a new definition to overcome and dethrone all others.

Only allow me to point out that I intend to operate with what is actually there, understanding that every definition of this type owes much to the historical circumstances in which it is formulated and, fundamentally, to who elaborates it and puts it into practice. Based on this, I intend to sketch some ideas that I trust can express and reflect the aspirations of many of us.

In spite of the ethnohistorical, political and socioeconomic differences among its units, since the 1970s there has been imposed, chiefly for political reasons, the geopolitical concept of the CARIBBEAN BASIN as a dominant definition. The formulation of this concept lies in a geopolitical, strategic and military perception of the region and responds, primarily, to the interests of the hemispheric hegemonic power. From this perspective, the CARIBBEAN BASIN, regardless of the differences that separate the continent from the islands and the countries of the Central American isthmus from North America and South America, constitutes one region, whose importance is rooted in the access to relevant mineral resources, to crucial sea lanes, to investments and economic benefits, but especially in the fact that it constitutes a "front yard" or "back yard" or, more precisely, the southeast flank of the United States.

This situation, which historically engendered "doctrines" and "corollaries" that justified North American hegemony in the area, has been strengthened by the good offices of President Ronald Reagan, from the beginning of the present decade. In this view, the conception of CARIBBEAN BASIN has been legitimized in terms of the strategic objectives of the U.S., not only in relation to the incarnations of the global confrontation, but as a sequel to the historical aim of this country to keep all extrahemispheric powers out of the region. From this perspective, the principal preoccupation is political stability in the Caribbean Basin states as a basic guarantee against the eventual penetration of external powers.

Geostrategic reasoning has defined us and homogenized us to the point where the concept Caribbean Basin has found its equivalent, in the context of the political rationality that the East-West conflict has imposed on us, in the KARIBIISKI BASEIN coined by the Soviets. The definition that this rationality establishes is marked, not by dreams, but by nightmares. The violent confrontations among men of the same color or of different races and languages; the nightmare of hunger and poverty brought on by these confrontations; the nightmare of submission and indifference to the pillage of our peoples and countrysides. It is this rationality whose historical logic speaks to us of war and extermination, of gratuitous suffering to benefit foreign interests, of grief and destruction of hopes.

Paradoxically, our definitions also respond to a logic of power, albeit slightly unrealistic. We define ourselves as LATIN AMERICANS, WEST INDIANS or ANTILLEANS, or as French, Dutch, British, or American, in accordance with the latitude where we were born, where our forefathers settled (often by force), and where we learned to speak our language, paying little or no attention to other identities that may not be based on culture or political history. So that geography fluctuates to the rhythm of history and political circumstances, and definitions that we use as our own reflect the divisions imposed on the region by colonial rivalries.

But up to what point are we mere objects of the history of the metropolis and up to what point is our history our prison, as Caryl Phillips certainly affirms in speaking of the "European tribe?" (Faber and Faber, London, 1987, p. 121.)

Perhaps our destiny is to suffer the divisive definitions imposed by former colonial powers, with the old layout of ethnic profiles and socioeconomic and political-institutional differences, or else the uniform geostrategic conception of the present with its taste of Coca Cola and McDonalds that mixes us up into the "global village," erasing our uniqueness?

We owe ourselves then a definition of our own, and, in this context, we owe to ourselves the realization of our own historical aspirations, despite the fact that the definitions used are, in the final analysis, those that come from interaction with "others." Such has been the case with the self-definition of "Latin American" imposed on the continent. Such has been, most recently, the case with the definition of "Afro-Caribbean" used to describe the insular Caribbean. [These definitions represent] both a reaction to the definitions that the "others" imposed on us, and a rejection of the perceptions that qualified us in a set fashion, but at the same time a reply in the framework of interaction with those "others."

This is not the place to ponder the interactionist conceptions born in the warmth of social psychology, nor the different versions found in the field of international relations. But nowadays it is not possible to see ourselves, to define ourselves, to clarify ourselves, outside of the planetary network of interrelations and communications imposed on us by the "global village" and its conflictive dynamic—the confrontation between the superpowers. The issue is, however, with respect to whom and to what we define and identify ourselves.

Our unique definitions are not those that come from the realities imposed by the strategic interests of the superpowers or by the realities imposed by the critical versions that we forge from the situation. It is not only the "other," seen favorably or unfavorably, who defines us and who makes our desires clear. Since the 19th century, Latin America tried to go its own way, with difficulties and contradictions. The recent revitalization of democratic regimes and the aspirations of economic cooperation and political unity, with deficiencies and obstacles, seem to be becoming progressively crystallized in efforts like those of Contadora and the Group of Eight. For its part, the Caribbean, by its own routes, has sought its own path of autonomy and development, on the basis of experiences perhaps less traumatic but not for that less distinctive and brave, where Caricom, with its highs and lows, or, on a different scale, the OECS, have pointed out the way.

So that, away from the determinations and conditions imposed by global realities, a space has developed for hemispheric actors to convert themselves into legitimate actors, with a margin of autonomy progressively wider as seen in their international roles. Especially in the last few years, despite the constrictions imposed by external debt and economic difficulties, we have followed a path oriented towards the search for democratic stability and socioeconomic development of our peoples, and, in a detached manner, not withstanding circumstantial reverses, a search for greater autonomy and a more specific identity in the international arena.

This general orientation of our societies, more or less jointly observed, has not freed us, of course, from the obvious contradictions and ambiguities imposed on us by our aspirations toward autonomy and the crude reality of the dependence of our economies. Among these contradictions and ambiguities our peoples have navigated, as all young people, fighting against adolescent fantasies and the powerful realities of the international system. However, recent events show that from the confusion there emerges, each time more clearly, a most pragmatic vision of our situation.

We have learned that to forge societies of egalitarian political participation and economic distribution is not the act of a single day, heroic but not for that less brief, and that to articulate democracy and development in a world full of threats and outside interference is not easy and requires perspicacy, common sense and the skill of our political leaders in order not to submit to the cruel dynamic of the global confrontation. Illustrations abound. Enough to cite Grenada in 1983 to know what I am referring to. But these requirements, with their pragmatic immediacy, cannot have far-reaching meaning if, at the same time, they are not led by the images that dreams, rather than nightmares, dictate.

From the 1970s, the international system has gradually been undergoing significant transformations. The hegemonic decline and recomposition of the U.S., the winds of change that have brought *perestroika* in the U.S.S.R. and its effects on Soviet foreign policy, the advances in European integration and the growing world standing and economic influence of Japan, to cite only the most important actors on the international scene, have provoked the obsolescence of the bipolar system, dominant in the years after World War II. The dilution of the bipolar scheme that kept the world geopolitical dynamic rigid in the 1950s, has not only opened up a space to the active presence of other industrialized actors, but also has introduced substantial changes in the capacities for autonomy and negotiation of the peripheral states. In such a way that unilateral definitions and policies are having less and less sway in the international system, especially since the weaker and smaller states learned to use international forums and agencies where, frequently, their votes are decisive for the interests of the great powers. Proof of that is the signing of the Panama Canal Accords in 1977 by Torrijos and Carter, in a situation that would have been inconceivable decades before, and also the recent inability of the American government to displace General Noriega from power. Instead, we are seeing, in other latitudes, situations unimagined in previous years, such as the Soviet withdrawal from Afghanistan. In sum, the question arises whether all these changes in the international system mark the end of the omnipotence of the great powers.

Without speculating on the outcome of these transformations, it is undeniable that a progressively larger space is being opened up so that the peripheral states can widen their margin of political autonomy and clamor for new definitions of their situation. In fact, this means that the space for dreams and aspirations which historically were denied, is being widened. But this affirmation implies fundamentally that the recourse to reproaches and historical blame has been closed, and that a greater autonomy implies greater responsibilities for ourselves.

This situation probably demands new approaches and innovative methods in our approximation of international reality that will also mean new definitions of our identity, to suit the new forms of interaction that might be established. But these new forms will also owe their quota to our participation and to our disposition to perceive in another way not only our "protectors" but also our neighbors, and to interact with them in a planet increasingly more linked by a complex system of interdependence. And this leads us to consider, in a particular way and in view of the changing regional and hemispheric circumstances, the relations among two groups of nations that historically have ignored each other. I am speaking of the "indifferent neighbors" of the Caribbean and Latin America, respectively, and of their relations in the context of a changing world geopolitical reality, and I am speaking of the new regional definitions that these relations demand.

In this sense, in the 1980s the process of democratic reconstitution of many Latin American countries has been articulated with a continental tradition of pacific resolution of interstate conflicts that, compared to other regions of the world, is grounded in a precedent that is difficult to eradicate. This precedent, based on the principle of nonintervention and respect for international law, has been reaffirmed by numerous regional initiatives such as that taken by Contadora and by the South American Commission for Peace, Regional Security and Democracy. In this context, one of the most virulent interstate conflicts to occur in the hemisphere in recent years is very much attributable to the coming together of two factors: the aspiration of the Argentine military to hold on to its illegitimate abuse of power in the country; and the clever political utilization of megalomania on the part of the government of Margaret Thatcher in Great Britain, producing a confrontation that involved, for the first time in many years, the participation of an extrahemispheric power in a continental war.

Paradoxically, in this perspective and not withstanding the general tendency towards political instability manifested by the regional actors, what has most tended to divide us has been the inheritance of unresolved colonial conflicts and the mutual lack of trust that our colonizers left us. In fact, although the conflict in the South Atlantic did not bring "West Indians" and Latin Americans to war, it served to strengthen our distances and our suspicions and mutual prejudices. Of course, the existence of unsettled boundary disputes, chiefly between Venezuela and Guyana and between Belize and Guatemala, reaffirmed the existing disunity, despite the thirdworldist leanings of leaders like Manley, Perez, or Echeverria in the 1970s, or the action of agencies of cooperation such as SELA.

To these objective facts, we must add, however, the mutual prejudices and preconceptions that we have inherited. Linguistic, institutional, racial and cultural differences in intellectual traditions that our colonizers generously left us have penetrated our own vision of our neighbors and have contributed to the magnification and enlargement of the existing foci of tension, converting them into dark threats.

Nevertheless, among the existing prejudices, there stands out also the perception that the neighbors are more unstable and can adversely affect the political situation of the region. Curiously, in the so-called BASIN we seem to forget, by and by, that the majority of states of the English-speaking Caribbean, for example, have an established tradition of democracy similar, despite the institutional differences, to that of

Venezuela, Mexico, and Colombia. And that both groups of nations, despite their differences, profess an identical preoccupation with the security and stability of the region.

In this sense, to widen the margin of autonomy of our states probably implies beginning to perceive our neighbors in their true dimensions and not under the illusion of inherited stereotypes. Instead, the widening of these margins before the dynamic imposed by the East-West confrontation and the geostrategic interests of external actors, can only be the result of cooperation and collaboration among the hemispheric actors. And this cooperation and collaboration can only be the consequence of the interest of these actors in the creation of conditions for the stabilization of democratic forms of coexistence that will bring with it the possibility of overcoming the economic obstacles that engulf our societies.

It is difficult to bring up the theme of cooperation and agreement, in particular between the Caribbean and the Latin American continent, when all previous experiences rather tend to point to the frustrations inherent in this type of initiative.

In Latin America, the initiatives for economic cooperation taken in the past—ALADI, ALALC, CACM, Andean Pact— have not produced the expected results. In the Caribbean, CARICOM has been restricted to the English-speaking states, and has kept in suspension the entry of Haiti, Surinam, and the Dominican Republic. Both CARICOM and the OECS have gone from crisis to crisis. However, the OECS seems interested in a political integration scheme for the Eastern Caribbean. Among the main obstacles faced by these organizations, the differences in actual and potential economic development of their members, along with the competition for external markets, have presented some of the most stubborn obstacles for success.

Paradoxically, except for some lukewarm initiatives of

cooperation between the Andean Pact countries and CARICOM, the schemes of economic cooperation and integration have been mutually exclusive between Latin America and the Caribbean. Differences of size, human and natural resources, and level of industrialization have contributed to this situation. Again, the commercial linkage between both regions, although significantly increased both in absolute value and in terms of share of world trade, remains restricted to a limited number of Caribbean and Latin American countries, among other reasons because of the lack of an adequate transportation and communications infrastructure.

But besides these objective situations, differences and mutual prejudices have combined to widen the distance. In fact, the organs of regional cooperation in which both the Caribbean and Latin America have been involved, such as CEPAL and, better yet, SELA, frequently have tapped the existing divergences and tensions.

Nevertheless, despite these divergences, one can point to such agreements for assistance and cooperation as the Pact of San Jose, promoted by Mexico and Venezuela, or the participation of these two countries and Colombia in the Caribbean Development Bank, or the most recent accords between these Latin American countries as well as Brazil and CARICOM on matters of fishing, technical assistance and agricultural cooperation, programs of industrial assistance and cultural exchange initiated in the last decade. In this sense, particular multilateral accords dealing with specific aspects of assistance and cooperation, have been more effective than broad bilateral schemes that open the way to other forms of agreement.

In fact, it is evident that the road to economic cooperation is paved with good intentions but, at the same time, a lot of difficulties inherent in the characteristics of the productive structures of the countries of the region, structures which are in many instances oriented to developing or expanding similar products and to exporting to the same markets, generally in the industrialized countries.

But more significant in these cooperative and interactive experiments have been the plans for organized political collaboration. In spite of the agreement on themes such as decolonization, anti-racialism, anti-apartheid or the promotion of a New International Economic Order in international forums and organizations, the host of divergent interests and tensions inherited from a colonial past has systematically appeared. Consequently, the Caribbean and Latin American blocs have functioned, with rare exceptions, like separate blocs within the international system.

This is a very curious situation, if we take into consideration the common aspirations for a greater degree of autonomy on the hemispheric and international scene. Particularly curious if we take into account that the games of economy and world power oblige us, within a branching and vertical structure, to interact actively with the industrialized states and ignore or depreciate immediate neighbors, mired in similar problems to ours. A curious situation if to this framework we add the tensions introduced by external intervenors, such as occurred during the unfortunate South Atlantic crisis when an abyss opened between both groups of nations in the OAS and the United Nations.

And nevertheless, the aspirations for autonomy of each group of nations demand, for the sake of these aspirations for autonomy and a relative margin of independent action, that we interact and communicate, establish alliances and forge mutual positions, and search for common regional solutions, initiatives that can only be realized through mutual recognition and a common voice on problems of underdevelopment. And this can only succeed through a major political agreement and commitment that seem most appropriate at this time and place.

However, maturity and pragmatism dictate caution and

moderation given the tumultuous whirlwind of changes within the international system. Past experience points to the necessity of cutting back on excessive ambitions and immature dreams and searching for the shelter of powerful protectors. But these self-imposed limitations and the search for paternal protection from the strong have led us, until now, to submerge ourselves in the forest of global conflict, forgetting, with relative ease, our own aspirations and dreams, without seeing, generally, any benefits to our societies.

Will there ever come the time then when we can bring together our efforts and our dreams? Will the right time come when we can define ourselves from our own perspective and identify our expectations and hopes?

PEACE AS PRETEXT AND GOAL

The strictly geostrategic definition of the region is a task that, in a special way, suggests questions and opens channels for reflection. However, we have tacitly taken the definition for granted, and so we debate it and its preoccupation with regional security and political stability in our societies. In the last few years, studies and analyses of the arming and the militarization of the region have proliferated.

However, to begin to consider our region from a perspective of peace, not only must the relations among regional actors change but also we must open up the possibility of other definitions, producing a significant change in our own conceptualization and, eventually, in our understanding of the area. In fact, more and more the climate is beginning to be ripe for a complete understanding of the vital importance of the democratic equation, peace and development. Permit me to speak simply so that clarity is not lost.

Only the stabilization of democratic systems will allow us to reduce armaments and the militarization of the societies of the region. This reduction is the precondition for the establishment of regional peace. At the same time, this reduction, given the economic difficulties being experienced by our societies, will permit us to spend our efforts and resources on promoting economic development.

This equation is gathering growing strength in the aspirations of the region, to the point that some leaders and regional and international organizations have begun to work concretely on the necessity of converting the Caribbean into a zone of peace.

Before he died, Errol Barrow pointed out, in an abrupt departure from some dominant orientations in the region, his desire that the territory of Barbados not be used to intimidate any neighbor, be it Cuba or the United States. In so doing, he emphasized the necessity of converting the Caribbean into a zone of peace.

Similar aspirations have been expressed by twenty-six Latin American and Caribbean states in the declaration approved in Quito in January 1984, and by South American political leaders in a meeting of the South American Commission for Peace, Regional Security and Democracy, held in Buenos Aires in April 1987. They postulated the urgency of converting the South American continent into a peaceful zone, free of territorial conflicts and of the effects of the East-West confrontation.

And along the same lines are the hopes openly expressed in the recent accords of Esquipulas and also the process of peace advanced by Nicaragua which builds on the Central American Contadora initiatives and those of the Group of Eight.

As a group, these initiatives come together in the Caribbean region, the point of departure of the aspirations for peace in the hemisphere given the growing preoccupation with regional security since the 1970s. In the Caribbean Basin the aspirations for peace of the Central American countries are interlaced with those of the Caribbean and South America, and their effective materialization requires bringing them all together. In this sense, a definition that unified us through common interests has been converted into a useful basis for recreating our coincidences and for postulating the establishment of zones of peace along the length and breadth of our hemisphere.

But is this a possible dream?

One of the first promoters of the idea of converting the Caribbean into a zone of peace was Eric Williams who, in a speech delivered in December 1983, stated, "If there is any justice in heaven, the area which has the just claim to being declared a zone of peace is the Caribbean area, which has for so long been afflicted by the machinations and manoeuvres, the hot wars and the cold wars, of the great powers and superpowers."

Fifteen years later, a formal proposal to establish such a zone in the Caribbean was made on the initiative of Grenada in October 1979 during the 12th plenary session of the General Assembly of the Organization of American States held in La Paz. On that occasion a resolution was approved, aimed at repudiating the view of the region as the sphere of influence of any power. It emphasized its support for ideological pluralism and peaceful coexistence, and called for all states to recognize the region as a zone of peace. The English-speaking Caribbean states in particular showed on that occasion their full support for the resolution. However, the resolution was not put into practice despite this approval.

Nevertheless, the original idea was taken up again by the Foreign Ministers of the member states of Caricom during their sixth meeting held in Grenada from June 30 to July 1, 1981. As a result, a working group was formed and met for the first time in Belize in March 1982. The Heads of Government meeting of Caricom in Ocho Rios, Jamaica, also promoted the activities of the working group which analyzed the possible options for a regional security treaty linked to the establishment of a zone of peace. In spite of this intiative, no subsequent action has been taken.

On the other hand, the initiative stressed the principles of nonintervention and ideological and political pluralism promoted by Caricom and eventually supported by other countries in the region. The invasion of Grenada put these principles into question but despite this there has remained, as an initial document to be considered, the proposals presented at the meeting in Belize. Among them, adherence to the principles of nonintervention and peaceful settlement of disputes stand out, as well as the need to strengthen the bonds and the existing cooperation among the states of the Basin, the liberation of colonial and externally dominated territories in the region, the prohibition of the establishment of new military bases and the dismantling of those already existing, the interdiction of all support and financing of mercenary groups, and the prohibition of the installment or maintenance of nuclear arms.

But not only have some governments of the region explicitly shown their support for the establishment of a zone of peace in the Caribbean—recent examples are Trinidad and Tobago, Barbados, and Venezuela—but also this initiative has received the support of diverse non-governmental organizations and broad social sectors.

To cite only one example, in April 1982 the Caribbean Council of Churches (CCC), which subsumes the main religious organizations in the region, adopted a resolution asking Caricom to consider "the establishment of a zone of peace in the Caribbean, including the ratification of any treaty that may be necessary to ensure this." Subsequently, a recent assembly of the CCC reiterated this position by way of

CCC concern about the growing militarization of the region and the presence of the superpowers, together with the impact of the Central American crisis on Caribbean societies. This proposal of the CCC meeting held in Barbados in 1986 was supported by the then Prime Minister of that country, Errol Barrow, who criticized the United States for attempting to convert Caribbean states into "client states" with some kind of access to North American goods and markets, and the USSR for trying to "afghanistanize" the region and use the Caribbean as a missile base in the policy of confrontation between the two superpowers.

The position assumed by Barrow coincided with his questioning, along with other Caribbean leaders such as James Mitchell, of the attempt to establish a regional security force and marks a frank return, after the events in Grenada, to nonalignment, ideological pluralism, and the principle of nonintervention traditionally held by Caricom.

In this sense, there has been a resurgence among the governments of the member states of Caricom, after the events in Grenada and the limitations shown by the Caribbean Basin Initiative, of a tendency to assume centrist positions and aspirations to nonalignment in foreign policy, with an emphasis on regional solutions to problems which, at the socioeconomic level, are characteristic of the Caribbean. In general, a more pronounced orientation towards avoidance of involvement in the East-West confrontation can be discerned, as seen in the attempts to strengthen regional initiatives within Caricom and to seek valid spokespersons in terms of technical cooperation and assistance in the former colonial metropoles, in Canada and in the Latin American countries. On the other hand, on par with the dilution of all effective military influence from Cuba in the area, pragmatic positions are being developed vis-a-vis the United States, which is assumed to be a decisive regional geopolitical force.

Also, in this context, there is beginning to emerge a consensus on the need to develop a new approach to the treatment of regional security which would both avoid excessive dependence on North American military assistance and also ensure that crises such as the Grenada one do not recur. This approach goes back to the traditional emphasis of the political elite of the English-speaking Caribbean on harmonizing a policy of regional security with a drive towards economic development and the consolidation of democratic systems.

In essence, one of the main threats to democratic stability and regional unity resides precisely in the inability of governments to implement development strategies that can adequately deal with the economic crisis, the foreign indebtedness, and the social tensions caused by increasing unemployment, particularly among the young population.

On the other hand, this aspiration is of necessity linked to impetus towards forms of regional cooperation that would incorporate new actors, not only at the economic level but also eventually at the level of political agreements, by way of generating collective responses to the economic crisis which affects Latin America and the Caribbean equally, and in order to reinforce the democratic processes as a guarantee of peace.

In this context, the spread in the English-speaking Caribbean of the idea of declaring a zone of peace in the Caribbean not only aims, at the level of regional security, at avoiding a new situation like the one that occurred with the invasion of Grenada, but also at reducing all possibility of other emerging conflicts, especially with Latin American nations that maintain territorial claims with some states of the non-Hispanic Caribbean.

On their part, for the Latin American states and, especially, for the nations of South America, the possibility of the establishment of a zone of peace in the Caribbean can respond to some of the prevailing interpretations of the regional situation in terms of North-South relations, by opening up simultaneously the possibility of guaranteeing a stability which would ensure their own security interests in the region. In this sense, the recent improvements in relations between Venezuela and Guyana and the redirection of their boundary dispute to a decision based on the mechanisms to be used for its solution by the Secretary-General of the United Nations, constitute events that can result in the disposition of both parties to the establishment of peace at the regional level. However, one element that could make Latin American support for this initiative difficult is tied to the perception of the Cuban presence as a threat to their interests, mainly in the cases of Venezuela, Colombia, and Brazil. The evolution of the situation of Cuba in the Latin American sphere, with the proposal made at the last meeting of the Group of Eight in Acapulco for a reincorporation of this country into the Latin American community, could constitute, however, an encouraging sign.

In this regard, the guidelines suggested by the document presented by Grenada at the meeting in Belize could show the way towards the establishment of a zone of peace in the region, with the effective support of the Latin American states, especially by considering as basic orientations of this initiative the principles of nonintervention and peaceful settlement of disputes traditionally promoted by the Latin American community.

In principle, in South America, the proposals for the establishment of a South American zone of peace, such as those expressed in April in the document of the South American Peace Commission, not only converge, in general terms, with the enunciation and promotion of those principles, but also point to the creation of a climate of regional confidence through the solution of intraregional conflicts and nonintervention so as to avoid the regionalization and internationalization of armed conflicts. On the other hand, these proposals also call for the limitation of military expenditure and for arms control, for the definitive denuclearization of the region, and the elimination of factors that contribute to the involvement of the region in global conflict. In particular, their proposals emphasize the elimination of foreign military bases and the prevention of any new extra-regional military presence and, particularly, the peaceful and negotiated solution of conflicts in Central America and the Caribbean.

In essence, both documents underscore the fact that any procedure for the establishment of a zone of peace would imply basically four fundamental measures:

- the withdrawal of all military bases and forces of external regional actors;
- the effective operationalization of the process of demilitarization on the basis of the Treaty for Non-Nuclear Proliferation of Tlatelolco;
- the implementation of a regional policy of arms control and disarmament, and
- the acceptance of the zone of peace statute for the respective regions by both global and regional powers.

So that both in South America and in the non-Hispanic Caribbean there is evolving a growing predisposition, on the part of governmental and non-governmental sectors, towards the establishment of measures aimed at creating a zone of peace.

In the case of the Caribbean, the growing regional disposition towards this type of initiative faces, however, a series of obstacles that are predominantly extra-regional in character. Among them, the following stand out:

- the reluctance of the United States to reduce its influence and control over regional security, so long as the area of the Caribbean Basin is considered a zone of vital hegemonic

ZONE OF PEACE: POSSIBILITY OR UTOPIA? 213

influence and Cuba continues to be seen as an effective threat to that influence;
- the resistance of the former colonial powers towards effectively withdrawing from the region due to the persistence of their strategic interests;
- the reluctance of the Latin American states that maintain border conflicts with Caribbean states to weaken their military situation vis-a-vis other neighboring states; and
- the difficulties, once the previous obstacles are overcome, in implementing adequate mechanisms for the conversion of the Caribbean into a zone of peace.

From this perspective, vis-a-vis the Central American crisis and its interpretation in light of the global confrontation with the USSR, the United States would have a hard time, at least in the short term and after having reasserted its hegemony over the Caribbean islands, accepting a zone of peace in what it considers to be an area of fundamental influence for reasons of strategy and prestige. The analysis of this situation, however, must take into account the crisis of consensus that is affecting the North American political system, particularly as evidenced by the highs and lows of the politics of the U.S. toward Central America. Eventually, in the medium term, once the presidential elections in the United States are concluded and in the context of the deepening of the negotiations on global disarmament, there may be an overcoming, albeit partial, of this obstacle, especially if the process of Central American peace continues to advance. Instead, the decisive factors to estimate would relate to the disposition of the U.S.S.R. to abandon its installations and personnel in Cuba and, with the concurrence of that country, accept a process of disarmament and control which could eventually leave it defenceless in the face of a North American threat. While the change in the foreign policy of the USSR towards the region and the Third World in general, in the context of the Soviet withdrawal from Afghanistan and the U.S. proposal for a suspension by both parties of the sending of arms to Central America, augurs well for a favorable disposition towards declaring a zone of peace in the Caribbean, the attitude of Cuba may be conditioned by distinct factors. Nevertheless, the possibility of a demilitarization of the Cuban society and a reorientation of resources and efforts towards other pressing necessities, could turn into an important inducement for a positive attitude towards the initiative. In any event, the position of Cuba would have to be evaluated also in light of the growing disagreement over the internal processes of the U.S.S.R. and its foreign policy as well as a series of fluctuating internal political factors. In this context, effective action by the regional actors is not to be underestimated, action aimed at contributing to overcoming the reluctance of all parties.

While not creating obstacles of the same magnitude as those mentioned earlier, the possible attitudes of the former metropolitan countries should also be considered. In this regard, Britain, Holland, and France present different problems. Whereas Holland wants a speedy withdrawal from the region, Britain maintains a presence in its associated dependencies. The persistence of the Malvinas conflict imposes in this latter case a strategic presence that is difficult for the United Kingdom to negotiate. Likewise, as long as the conflict between Guatemala and Belize persists, Britain will maintain, even if in a reduced and partial manner, a military contingent on Belizean territory or, at best, will accept its substitution by some type of North American presence. In the case of France, the permanence of its military bases and personnel is closely linked to its strategic interests in French Guiana (which certainly also implies an interest on the part of other European states that participate in the Ariane Aerospace Project), and with France not belonging to NATO. All of this makes France's position difficult to change in the con-

ZONE OF PEACE: POSSIBILITY OR UTOPIA? 215

text of the regional geopolitical dynamic and basically dependent on the country's participation in the global system. This situation has contributed to the non-ratification by this European actor of Protocol No. 1 of the Tlatelolco Treaty. In more immediate terms, the eventual overcoming of Latin American reluctance seems more feasible, given that the solution of Venezuela's claim to the Essequibo, although it has not significantly advanced, has given rise to a noticeable improvement in the relations between this country and Guyana. Again, recent information indicates that the Guatemalan government appears inclined to initiate a dialogue with the government of Belize as regards their continuing border conflict. Notwithstanding these encouraging signs, neither of the two conflicts appears ready to be resolved in the short or medium terms. There are also persistent border tensions in the region between Venezuela and Trinidad and Tobago, Venezuela and Colombia, and Guyana and Suriname, to cite only the most outstanding, which may affect any aspiration towards a process of disarmament. A similar case is presented in the relations between Haiti and the Dominican Republic. Cuba, in turn, in spite of the results of Grenada, continues to be a factor of concern, not only to North American interests but also for Latin American states such as Colombia and Venezuela both in terms of internal political factors (for Colombia) and in terms of the concern for ensuring political stability in the region (for both countries). Despite these situations, the implementation of a zone of peace in South America can become a positive factor for the implementation of a similar process in the Caribbean. Likewise, the easing of the Central American crisis can create the conditions under which actors such as the U.S. and the Latin American states can accept, in principle, the establishment of a zone of peace in the Caribbean region.

Reciprocally, the establishment of a situation of this nature in the Caribbean would facilitate the implementation of a similar initiative in South America, where the main obstacles reside in the persistence of intraregional conflicts. Again, a zone of peace in the Caribbean would contribute to the deepening of relations between the region and the Latin American states, not only at the level of economic cooperation but also in terms of the modalities of political agreements which would enhance the capacity for negotiation of both regions in the international arena. However, in this scenario, a fundamental conditioning element is, of course, the evolution that may follow the process of peace in Central America.

Finally, one of the main problems resides not only in the disposition of this group of actors to accept the establishment of a zone of peace in the Caribbean, but in its formulation and implementation by a regional or international organization able to guarantee its effective functioning. I leave in the hands of the specialists the discussion, in this regard, of the viability of the United Nations, with the decisive political weight exercised in this body by the superpowers; of the Organization of American States, given the successive crises which it has undergone; of Caricom, with its experience in the coordination of foreign policies but its limitation of restricting its membership to the English-speaking Caribbean states; or of any other regional or international body. Fundamentally, the difficulties revolve around the mechanisms to be implemented for an effective conversion of the Caribbean into a zone of peace while avoiding the problems that confronted the creation of a similar zone in the Indian Ocean.

In this context, the obstacles cited can only be overcome, however, through the will and coordinated action, both at the regional and international levels, of the main protagonists involved in this initiative, namely the Caribbean states. But for this coordination to be produced, these must exist: a common awareness that the resolution of the problems of regional security implies, as a precondition, the solving of the region's basic socioeconomic problems which are the main cause of the situations of political instability and vulnerability that the societies of the Caribbean and Latin America confront, and the possibility of developing, in an autonomous but at the same time regionally coordinated manner, the most appropriate strategies for overcoming these problems.

From this perspective, the aspirations to regional peace cannot be the exclusive prerogative of political leaders and governments, but demand also the agreement of political parties, religious associations, trade unions, business associations, youth bodies, women's groups, professional associations, artists' groups, peace movements, and human rights bodies. In sum, all those social actors who can make this region a redoubt of peace, including, especially, academics. And this is the challenge that, as members of the CSA, pertains to us particularly.

In essence, and to conclude, a new definition of the region from the perspective of peace and on the basis of coordinated regional action, not only of governmental but also, principally, of social and nongovernmental actors, is the new challenge that, perhaps in a utopian way, our commitment to the region presents us.

Finally, I hope that you can forgive these expectations and ideas—perhaps naive and utopian—that I wanted to share with you tonight. But an imaginative poet was on the right track when he said, "Utopias are frequently no more than premature truths."

NOTES

1. This article was translated by J. Braveboy-Wagner, former editor of the Caribbean Studies Association Newsletter. We used the translated version of the address as it was presented in

several issues of the CSA Newsletter. Footnotes and references were eliminated and references were not cited.

BRIEF BIOGRAPHY

NAME Andres Serbin

DATE OF BIRTH September 1, 1948

ACADEMIC DEGREES Ph.D. Universidad Central de Venezuela, Venezuela, 1987

M.S. Universidad Simon Bolivar, Venezuela, 1978

B.A. Universidad de la Plata, Argentina, 1974

ACADEMIC AFFILIATIONS Director, Instituto Venezolano de Estudios Sociales y Politicos (INVESP) Caracas.

Professor of Sociology and International Relations; Dircctor, Venezuelan Institute of Social and Political Studies; CSA President, 1987-1988

BOOKS *Indigenismo y autogestion*, (Co-editor) Monte Avila, Caracas, 1980

Geopolitica de las relaciones de Venezuela con el Caribe (Ed.) Fondo Editorial Acta Cientifica, Caracas, 1983

Venezuela y las relaciones internacionales en la Cuenca del Caribe, ILDIS/AVECA, CARACAS, 1987

Nacionalismo, etnicidad y politica en la Republica Cooperativista de Guyana, Bruguera, Caracas, 1981

Etnicidad, clase y nacion en la culture politica del Caribe de hable inglesa Academia Nacional de la Historia, Caracas, 1987.

El Caribe: zone de paz? Geopolitica integracion y seguridad en el Caribe no-hispanico, Nueva Sociedad/Comision Subamericana de Paz, Caracas, 1989

Etnocentrismo y geopolitica. Percepciones y relaciones entre America Latina y el Caribe de hable inglesa, Academia *Etnocentrismo y geopolitica. Percepciones y relaciones entre America Latina y el Caribe de hable inglesa*, Academia Nacional de la Historia, Caracas, 1989

SELECTED ARTICLES

"La Evolucion Postcolonial del Caribe Anglofono y Holandes: El Socialismo Caribeno y Las Nuevas Alternativas Politicas," in Juan Tokatlian and Klaus Schubert (Eds.): *Relaciones internacionales en la Cuenca del Caribe y la politica exterior de Colombia*, FESCOL/CAMARA DE COMERCIO DE BOGOTA, BOGOTA, 1982

"Guyana: Die Gewerkschaftsschiene," in R. Dunjaboy and Karl Hubener (Eds.): *Unterwanderung. Die Destabilisiering-Strategie del Usa von Angola bis Nicaragua*, Peter Hammer Verlag, Wuppertal, 1984

"Procesos Etnoculturales y Percepciones Mutuas en Las Relaciones Entre America Latina y El Caribe de Hable Inglesa", in *Journal of Latin American and Caribbean Studies* (Amsterdam), No. 39 June-Dec. 1985

"Autogestion Indigena O Co-Gestion Indi-genoestatal?," in F. Iturraspe (Ed.): *Participacion, congestion y autogestion en America Latina*, Nueva Sociedad, Caracas, 1986

"Les Conflits Interetatiques dans les Ameriques," in *Etudes Internationales* (Quebec), Vol. XVII, No.2 Juin 1986

"Venezuela Anti el Caribe Anglofono: Percepciones y Estilos Cognitivos," in *Homines* (San Juan), Vol. 11, No.1 April 1987, and in *Politica Internacional* (Caracas), vol. 2, No. 6, 1987.

Visions of Development Beckoning: The Caribbean Studies Association

J. E. GREENE

> Vision animates, inspires and transforms purpose into action. It articulates a view of a realistic, credible, attractive future for the Organisation. Vision is a target that beckons.
>
> *(Bennis and Nanus)*

The Caribbean Studies Association is fourteen years old. It therefore provides an opportunity to celebrate. Like in most celebrations, however, there is need for reflection on the past and a projection into the future. This activity of reflection is simultaneously intimidating. It is like a teenager faced with the challenges:

- of mixed emotions imposed by the transition from childhood to adulthood
- of anxieties about the road ahead
- of pressures to be a success
- of temptations to falter (and become a drop out)
- of ambivalence, even confusion, about available options that could make a difference
- of the traumas of just growing up.

Yet it is in the teens when the aspirations of being an adult loom large, when dreams are fashioned, ambitions moulded, goals set and visions beckon.

THE CSA FAMILY NEXUS

The Caribbean Studies Association is like a family whose ancestral moorings in the Aborigines, Africa, Asia and Europe are reflected in the multi-racial, multi-cultural, multi-linguistic gathering assembled today. Like many Caribbean families, the identity of the CSA permeates the metropolitan centres with "permanent residence" providing essential links and lifelines in Washington, New York, Miami, Toronto, Montreal and London. Like most West Indian families its network is extensive: its strengths are derived through the extended family which is a complex of class, colour, location; of experience, expressive style, interests and goals. The CSA meeting provides us with an opportunity — like Christmas or Carnival — to have a family reunion.

Like a true Caribbean family, it strengths and weaknesses are embedded in the form and substance of its diversity.

A teenager, or any one for that matter, enveloped in the kaleidoscopic environment of a CSA family is bound to be sensitive to the actual or potential conflicts in a scenario where some relatives assert their Hispanic supremacy: others despise the marginalisation of their Dutch and French heritage in spite of their perceived cultural superiority. Yet others display a pomposity, even conceit, of their British heritage regardless of colour or accent. But the same teenager, capable of looking beyond these social variances, may yet be intrigued by the processes of adjustment that bring accord or knit this complex of factions together in a real or imagined vision of development.

The Caribbean Studies Association by its focus and location in the Caribbean is bound to be concerned with the issues of development. Since the end of World War II and in particular in the 1950s, 1960s and 1970s, Europe's former colonial possessions acquired independence and emerged as new states with new frontiers. Even in the case of the French departments (Guadeloupe, Martinique) and in the Commonwealth of Puerto Rico, the aspiration is to become economically developed. This process is proving to be a difficult one as much for the larger Caribbean countries like Cuba, The Dominican Republic and Venezuela as for the medium sized states (like Jamaica, Belize, Guyana, Surinam, Trinidad and Tobago and Barbados) and the smaller states like those of the OECS territories; Aruba, Bonaire and Curacao; The Caymans, Turks and Caicos.

To tackle the complex problems facing us as a Caribbean Family we need to promote rather than stifle those among us with creative and visionary zeal. This reminds me of a sign posted on the Jamaican Institute for the Blind in Kingston: "many have sight but not vision".

DEVELOPMENT: A GLOBAL PERSPECTIVE

For almost two decades after World War II, Social Scientists aided and abetted the division of the world into "traditional" and "modern" societies. They also linked economic development to the concept of "modernization". Not only has the goal of modernization been remarkably elusive but the transformation from traditional to modern societies as an object of public policy is now widely recognized as being utopian. The chemistry of development, whether in Asia,

Africa or Latin America or the Caribbean reveals itself as an unstable compound of diverse political, social, cultural and intellectual elements, not to speak of many that may be termed economic. The conflicting institutional interests are so varied that any simple theory of nation-building, modelled on what occurred in the New World in the eighteenth century or the Old World in the nineteenth, seems quite inadequate.

Yet development continues to be the label that frames the hopes and aspirations of multitudes in the developing countries; that guides their nation-building efforts and inspires the international enterprise of development assistance. It is used as a point of reference in domestic and foreign policy by experts in almost every conceivable field: education, health, science and technology, industry, agriculture, social welfare, administration.

It is clear, however, that by the late 1960s sharp divergences in the concept and application of development had emerged. Third World voices were denouncing the whole international structure in which development was conceived. These Third World voices calling for a New International Economic Order fell on deaf ears. In the Western capitalist system the response was the resurgence of neo-classical market economics simultaneous with the declining role of government. They brought critical doubts about the statism of development and programs with clearly negative implications for the Third World.

A central paradox that haunted the founders of the postwar world systems (like the UN) more than four decades ago, is even more haunting today. The paradox relevant to Associations like ours is: how to reconcile amorphous ideas such as a "world community" and "global issues" when ethnocentricity and parochialism remain more attractive magnets for individual and group loyalty.

The elegant economist, Barbara Ward, vividly captures the

paradox of our time as the 'hinge of history' in which the biosphere of our inheritance and the technosphere of our creation are out of balance:

> The door of the future is opening onto a crisis more sudden, more global, more inescapable, more bewildering than ever encountered by the human species. And one which will take decisive shape within the life span of children who are already born. (Cleveland and Bloomfield)

She was writing in 1971. Everything that has happened since those words were written reinforces their prescient wisdom:

> —from the development of the atomic fission to that of the nuclear fission; from the capacity to produce large explosions to the evolution of complex industrial and military systems; from the cascading catastrophes marked by Bhopal and Chernobyl to that of the Challenger shuttle; from the life scientists' melding genetics and chemistry to the production of the recombinant DNA; from biotechnology's "gene revolution" leading to the increase in productivity of plants and animals; from proven ways to make human insulin from bacteria to new ways to make protein cheap and abundant; from practical ways for women to have fewer babies to potential ways to detect and correct inborn errors in metabolism and even for men to have babies.

These advances have also been accompanied by the build-up of carbon dioxide and other green-house gases in the global atmosphere. And then there is the explosive marriage of computers and telecommunications which is not only changing the global configuration but forcing nations to rethink the essence of their philosophies—economics based on scarcity, governance based on secrecy, laws based on exclusive ownership, management based on hierarchy.

In other words, in the short period of time since the CSA was born—between 1974 and the present time—there has been a massive surge in global interdependence that what in 1974 was regarded as a domestic problem is now automatically recognized as a global one.

CONTEMPORARY INDICATORS AND CONSTRAINTS

Just about the time when the CSA came into existence in the mid-1970s major developed countries began to confront their economies so as to deliberately forestall the effects of an oil price rise. This resulted in a severe global recession abruptly interrupting the industrialization process in developing countries at a crucial stage. It is argued in some quarters that the situation today is different in many respects and that a mild recession may even be a necessary evil.

According to the report of the OECD (1988), GDP growth in the USA is expected to drop to the 2.7 percent level in 1989 from the 2.9 percent average in the previous two years. The IMF foresees a gradual but definite slow-down in all the Group of Seven countries, reducing the Group's average growth rate from 3.1 percent in 1987 to 2.7 percent in 1989. At the same time, the IMF is projecting a constant 3 percent growth for the whole world economy for three years in succession, pinning its hopes on the improved performance by developing countries. [UNIDO, 1988] These are paralleled by the view from UNIDO of strong performances in Japan and Western European countries. While the sweeping reforms undertaken in Eastern Europe may have adverse effects on their immediate growth, this will have an impact on very very few developing countries.

What will, however, have an impact both on the Third and

the First World is the present posture of Soviet leadership which places emphasis on Perestroika: its objectives are radical economic reform and the democratization of party life and society. Perestroika, by creating an apparently new image of Socialism in the global system, has temporarily, at any rate, muted the orthodox forces of Communism. China's new commitment to market reforms in its economic programme has also reinforced this trend within the Communist world, with implications for the radicalism in the Third World that featured so prominently in the mid-70s when the Association came into existence.

This is the general international environment in which as a teenage Association we find ourselves grappling with visions of development. But these visions need to be further sensitized by immediate constraints that appear to be minimizing the options available to us:

- *Europe in 1992*
  First of all, there is the realization of the coming of the European Market. By 1992, this will be a single internal market without frontiers for promoting free movement of persons, goods, services and capital within the EEC.
- *Uruguay Round of Multi-Lateral Negotiations*
  This signals a trend toward the liberalization of trade with unprecedented tariff concessions across the board.
- *U.S.-Canada Free-Trade Agreement*
  The looming possibility of this phenomena is bound to erode even the marginal and unsatisfactory trade concessions for Caribbean goods entering those markets under CBI and CARIBCAN.

The major implication of these developments is that the Caribbean cannot fail to recognize that it enjoys more absolute and relative preferential access to a variety of international markets than any other grouping of developing countries.

- Under the Lome Convention it has extensive preferences to the EEC market of 320 Million.
- Under CBI it enjoys preferences in the US market of 260 Million.
- Under CARICOM, 26 Million in Canada. (Carrington, 1989)

The point at issue is that while these current arrangements are "oneway", the discussions taking place globally are placing emphasis, increasingly, on *reciprocity*.

THE CARIBBEAN DILEMMA

The oil price shocks of the 1970s have been superseded by the debt crisis of the 1980s which is now likely to be absorbed into the rising tide of protectionism by the industrialized countries envisaged on the horizons of the 1990s. The social, economic and cultural impact of this avalanche of global events is as ominous for the region as a whole as Hurricane Gilbert was for Jamaica. Yet Jamaica survived a "Wild Gilbert".

As far as the CARICOM region is concerned, the debt crisis was heightened by two factors:

(i) the high interest rate policies in the developed countries; and
(ii) the reduction of foreign lending by the advanced countries.

Between 1980–88 the debt service ratio grew rapidly in Dominica, Grenada, Montserrat, St. Kitts-Nevis in the OECS territories. In the same period, debt as a percentage of GDP grew spectacularly in Guyana, Jamaica and Trinidad and Tobago. The most outstanding case outside Guyana, which is now in a very special category, is Trinidad and Tobago where the debt/GDP ratio has jumped from 8 percent in 1983 to 22.4 percent in 1988. (COMSEC and CARICOM, 1988). The situation in the Spanish, Dutch and French Caribbean is virtually the same as for the CARICOM countries, except that in the case of Puerto Rico there is USA paternalism and for Gaudeloupe and Martinque, there is France. In addition to this overall picture, we need to note that for the CARICOM states:

- per capita incomes and consumption have largely fallen;
- the human costs of prolonged recession have been devastating;
- unemployment ranges from 17.5 percent in Trinidad and Tobago to over 30 percent in Guyana;
- that according to current projections unemployment for the CARICOM region as a whole is likely to move from 25 percent in 1980 to 32.1 percent in 1990 and climb even higher to around 36 percent by the end of the century;
- out-migration is likely to be reduced because of restrictive measures being increasingly resorted to in the main countries of destination, U.K., U.S.A. and Canada.

One major result of all these factors is the projected crisis of job opportunities by the Year 2000 especially for the young people in the 20-30 age group: the same group that are teenagers today. For them the alternative of finding employment abroad is likely to contract even further.

A fourteen year old Caribbean teenager forced to look more and more to the Caribbean and less to elsewhere for "the solutions" will tend to be intimidated by the prospects of growing up. Some comfort however is provided by John Mansefield:

in happiest childhood,
I could at once without effort

imagine, any needed scene
with brightness and detail
with what is called vision.

VISIONARY MODELS

All the signals suggest the need for visionary leadership. Are we in the CSA capable of/prepared for generating such visionary leadership? Are we ready? If we are we need to contemplate that visionary leaders should offer new strategies for survival and work through institutions: they should be as much organizers as orators, building institutions that become the means for individuals to achieve their goals. These institutions are intended to change people's daily behaviour and to project on the future the realization of the heavenly or worldly city of the vision. (Migdal, 1988:4) History has so far illustrated three main types of visionary leaders.

Villains

In his famous study *The Hero of History* Sidney Hook (1943) provides a model of individuals, often wicked, like Hitler and Mussolini, who left an imprint of their personalities on history but almost destroyed the world.

Heroes

They are event-making men: Caesar, Cromwell, Napoleon and Lenin. They all displayed exceptional qualities of leadership in freeing the path they had taken from opposition and placing themselves above the social class whose interests they actually or presumably served.

The Moses' (or Deliverers) of This World

They are recruited from among the humble and like Marcus Mossiah Garvey, Mahatma Gandhi and Martin Luther King remain part of the social unit they lead. This is why (according to Michael Keren, 1988: p. 70) we do not have one image of the Moses' of this world but rather diverse images developed through generations. The Hellenic world portrayed him as a philosopher king, Islam as prophet-Caliph, the Renaissance as a Zeus, Weimar-Germany as a blue-eyed redeemer of the nation and Hollywood as a tall, dark handsome man.

This raises the question, to what model of visionary must we subscribe and aspire?

I am intrigued by the concept "Visionary Realists" put forward by a group of political scientists writing recently on this subject. Operationally defined, the visionary realist:

> is neither a dreamer who ignores constraints posed by reality on the accomplishment of one's vision, nor a pragmatist overwhelmed by those constraints. He or she defines transformational goals, possibly exceeding those deemed feasible by others, and applies them to the complexities of the real world through the careful but straightforward use of power, knowledge and human decency. In a word, visionary realism is the creative pursuit of daring goals. It is leadership which differs from the common notion of charisma in three important ways. It stresses the effective implementation of vision rather than its appeal; considers the leader as part of the social order rather than a figure situated above that order; and conceives visionary realism not so much as a personal quality but as a behavioural trait that can be institutionalized. (Kevan, 1988:5)

PARAMETERS OF CARIBBEAN VISIONS

As we look to the future, it is first of all necessary for us as a CSA family to place some parameters on our visions of development. They must be identified with a specific set of values. These values must aid the formation of public policy, the primary aim of which ought to be that of increasing the social well being i.e. the quality of life of the society in general, the mass of deprived people in particular. Given the colonial history of the Caribbean, development is coterminous with decolonization. It is a process which aims at transforming the capabilities of former colonial societies. These capabilities are varied. In the first place, there is the question of technology, the relevance of which could provide the basis of enhancing the material well-being of any system. Relevant technology can provide the alteration of capital structures, innovations in economic organisation, more effective communications and increased productivity. Secondly, there is the question of skills. The urgency is to update them so as to maximize society's output. In the final analysis a society's capacity to increase its skill-quotient increases also the factors of production which can create new products. Third, relevant technology and increased skills are both related to the management of human resources and the environment. In other words, it is a measure of the effectiveness of man's capabilities to use innovative techniques and know-how to influence the development of his society.

For these reasons, if the activities of an Association like ours are to contribute to the transformation of Caribbean society they must begin with the transformation of the individual and this in turn raises a fourth capability viz, psychological development. Even with adequate technology and skills, a society may remain colonized if the values and attitudes of the individuals in that society are trapped in colonialism, reinforcing "the colonial mentality". It is this psychological capability that raises the specific objectives and kind of visionary framework in reference to which the development problems are tackled.

OPERATIONAL STRATEGIES FOR CSA

Building Capabilities

Having established what are the parameters of our visions of development, how can we as a CSA family strengthen our capabilities to apply the concept to our social reality?

First of all, that we make an annual pilgrimage and locate our family reunion in the Caribbean rather than in New York or Miami or Toronto or Montreal seems to be a recognition of the fact that the legitimate source and resonance of Caribbean studies reside in the region. As academics and policy makers within the CSA family, we need to ensure that this source of our being is fully capable of responding to our visions of development. In other words, we need to ensure that the source to which we come for reunion annually is not just a dalliance but a center of excellence. Hence, we need to establish the basis of the relationships, linkages, collaborative ventures between members of the CSA and their institutional affiliations in the North and South.

Centers of Excellence

Institutions of higher learning in the South—Universities in particular—invariably stem from Western models and function in a world system of higher education which is dominated by metropolitan institutions. Ali Mazuri (1975: 181-211) gives a vivid description of African universities as peripheral institutions in the international knowledge system. To a larger extent, until recently the generation and distribution of knowledge were dominated by institutions in the North. Centers of excellence presuppose pre-eminence in research and training, institutional recognition for outstanding work in particular fields of scholarly endeavors. However, to acquire and sustain such recognition requires infrastructure to accommodate and attract a cadre of scholars, whose reputations in turn enhance the knowledge distribution associated with the specific center. In this respect, an active programme of dissemination of knowledge emanating from scholarly research is a critical function of centers of Excellence. An active publications program— especially an in-house journal—seminars or internationally acclaimed workshops, are some of the more traditional features of these centers. In addition, centers of excellence tend to be associated with schools of thought or sources of innovation or creative activity.

Area Studies

Ironically, in the heyday of area studies in the 1960s, the most recognized centers of African, Asian, Latin American Studies, were located in metropolitan universities rather than in the respective continents. Links were established among Asia, Africa, Latin America and the Caribbean to facilitate large scale projects and to provide training at the Masters and Doctoral levels in specialized fields within area studies programs. In Britain, the Inter-University Council sponsored at Manchester University training at the doctoral level in Government and Public Administration from the University of the West Indies and universities of East Africa. The three-way link, England-Africa-Caribbean, provided exchange for both staff and students across the continents during 1966-1980. Among Canadian universities, McGill and Guelph admitted several candidates from Caribbean universities on a continuous basis in the Social Sciences and Agriculture respectively, while the University of Western Ontario was one of the major sponsors of the Department of Management Studies at UWI in the early 1970s providing for faculty exchanges and other forms of faculty development.

North/South Linkages

The largest of these area studies programmes is sponsored by US universities. The Carnegie Commission provided a most comprehensive report of these linkages up to the 1970s. It illustrates the variety of higher education training courses in international relations, discusses the curriculum and assesses the involvement of American universities and colleges in area and language studies, technical assistance, study abroad, faculty and student exchange and training and educational co-operation. These trends have apparently continued into the 1980s. What in particular has persisted into the present time is the use of Third World countries as laboratories for developmental research, while recognition for scholarly work in developing area studies is mostly credited to the Northern link. One of the leading centers in Tropical Medicine, for example, is located at London University; another for 'development studies' at Sussex University, and for Development Administration at Harvard University. The main reason is that much of the research on the respective topics is reported in Western journals and interpreted by Western scholars. Area studies centers in the Third World have been invariably sponsored by parent institutions in the North. These links, while mutually beneficial, may continue to be prejudicial to the development of excellence in the

South unless some attempt is made to indigenize the infrastructure for research and publications.

The CSA has a golden opportunity to help in arresting the dependency syndrome in the North/South linkage and to facilitate a greater emphasis on South/South linkages.

South/South Initiatives

There are several 'initiatives' in this regard in Latin America and the Caribbean. The Latin American Faculty of the Social Sciences (FLASCO) which commenced in the 1970s and the Consortium Graduate School in the Social Sciences of the Universities of the West Indies and Guyana inaugurated in 1985 are attempts at institutionalizing graduate programmes in the Social Sciences. They are both responses to the needs of their respected regions. Other Centers, attached to institutions in the region, have gained international recognition either because of the work of prominent scholars or schools of thought or because of the reputations they have established through sustained and high quality scholarly endeavours. The New World group and the Department of Economics, UWI, Mona, in the 1960s–1970s as well as the "Dependency School" in Latin America in the 1950s–1960s achieved this status. So too has the journal of *Social and Economic Studies*, the flagship of the Institute of Social and Economic Research, now in its 38th volume.

Caribbean Studies Programmes

While Centers of Excellence are obviously built-up around the work of individuals, they can only be maintained and sustained as part of a vision of institutional rather than personal development. As members of this CSA family, we each need to embark on a self-examination: 'What have I done or what am I doing or what can I do to help to build a Caribbean institution and to create a Center of Excellence in the Caribbean?'

There is a growing demand from various Centers, in particular in Canada, the United States of America and the United Kingdom, for general and specialized courses in Caribbean Studies. The expertise in Caribbean History, Literature, Linguistics, Sociology, Anthropology, Cultural Analysis as well as the Creative Arts and Sciences can be combined in programmes designed to respond to the various needs. An International Programme of Caribbean Studies being done as a collaborative venture between the Spanish, Dutch, French and English-speaking institutions of this region is one way to develop multi-disciplinary modules that would benefit from on-going research in Caribbean Studies, enhance the outreach capabilities of Caribbean universities and act as a catalyst for research that would address major gaps, including the fields of ethno-musicology, archaeology, the Creative Arts and linguistics.

Building such a facility in the Caribbean may in the short-run reduce the proliferation of individual short-term tours from the metropole that are conducted by genuine as well as "tourist" academics. In the long-run, it has the possibility of being a vibrant network, that places the collaborating institutions in the North as well as the South at the cutting-edge of thought and development in Caribbean Studies.

Multi-disciplinary Approaches to Development

This CSA family also has the utmost competence to facilitate the achievement of development imperatives through multi-disciplinary approaches.

It is clear that the economic models, in spite of Sir Arthur Lewis' monumental works, have not maximized the benefits to the Caribbean as a whole. It is not my intention at this stage to provoke a debate on the virtues or otherwise of Sir Arthur Lewis' contribution. There are 9 panels at this conference that are pursuing this endeavor. Never-the-less, it is worth noting that the veracity of Sir Arthur's vision was rooted in the fact that his economic models of development displayed a grasp of anthropology, sociology and politics and the humanities. Small wonder he was so greatly misunderstood in the Caribbean while South East Asia embraced his thought with the obvious manifestation in South Korea and Taiwan.

But I make this observation of Sir Arthur only to suggest that the Caribbean Studies Association has an opportunity to assert the primacy of the multi-disciplinary approaches to the understanding of and prescriptions for development. We need to place on the agenda more issue areas like poverty, rural development, entrepreneurship, health care, urbanization, technological change, that bring various disciplines together to explore the problematique as well as to grapple with the solutions.

Fourteen years of family history in the CSA and experiences from other families of Associations are sufficient to suggest that leaving the development visions in the hands of a single discipline is not working. *I am convinced that while our theory and historical understandings of our problems are adequate, it is our method of analysis that is faulty, i.e. we are approaching the multidisciplinary problems of development with unidisciplinary tools of analysis.*

Intra-Caribbean Approaches

We need also to provide the basis for greater linkages across the linguistic zones and collaborative approaches to the study of common problems like debt, unemployment, human resource capabilities, the role of the State, race and gender relations. The Association has made a tentative beginning in this respect by introducing at this meeting task forces on "scholarly publishing", "the role of higher education", "peace and security in the Caribbean".

Fourteen years of family history inform us that in spite of our pretentions we have not sufficiently enriched our pedigree by absorbing a greater number of our relatives in the Hispanic, French and Dutch Caribbean. Where are our Cuban brothers and sisters? Why are more Haitians not at our meetings or Martiniqueans or Surinamese? We have an opportunity to work toward broadening the intellectual and geopolitical base of this family. And in so doing we have an opportunity to demonstrate through visionary leadership and example that we truly understand the implications of "Europe 1992", "the Uruguay round" and the potential of a "US-Canadian free trade zone" for the future of the Caribbean. Are we prepared now as the New World Group was in 1962 to match our vision with action? *If so, all the indications demand that we must begin to work seriously (because time is running out) not only for the integration of the OECS territories, not only for a meaningful CARICOM but for a Caribbean and Latin American Community (CARLACOM). Given the international signals and regional symptoms, no other vision of development seems to make sense.*

THE ULTIMATE: A CARIBBEAN DIASPORA

This Association has the resources to ensure that its visions of development are anchored in the roots of the region as a whole. We are fortunate to have writers and poets within this Association who help us to interpret the expressive styles in our society, who help us to relate our abstract models to the views of the people. But one of the major weaknesses in our intellectual armory which is also reflected in the agenda of our Association is the lack of emphasis that we place on philosophy. *More particular, our vision of leadership must be reflected in a 'philosophy of hope': a philosophy which counteracts the psyching of small nations like ours into a resignation to subordinate status: political, social and economic; philosophy that reinforces a vision which offers a rare capacity to consider existing realities as transformed possibilities to inspire a collective image of a better future.*

This brings me to the final point. Our visions of development have been predominantly fashioned by adherence to one or other of the prevalent socio-economic and political models of change. With very few exceptions, these have been generated outside our real life experiences. They have for the most part neglected the philosophical and cultural dimensions of our being. There is a sense in which the indigenous culture must be recreated. The calypso, the rhumba, the reggae, the voodoo are significant in so far as they express feelings that represent critical factions and tendencies in our societies. Any plan for change must harness these elements of our folkways whether in prose, poetry, in song or in dance. These folkways can provide vital linkages with the revolutionary past illustrated by Toussaint (Haiti), Cuffy (Guyana), Bogle (Jamaica), Bolivar (Venezuela), Marti (Cuba), all ordinary people who helped to pioneer a consciousness of Caribbean roots and sensitize us to the common struggle that we as Caribbean people share. Our heroes have provided a useful lesson that we may wish to symbolize:

> Vision animates, inspires and transforms purpose into action. It articulates a view of a realistic, credible, attractive future for the Organisation. Vision is a target that beckons.

As a Caribbean family in the CSA, as scholars, as policymakers, as Caribeanists, for all the reasons that I have advanced, it seems to me (and I hope to you) that together we can be the architects of the ultimate vision. A CARIBBEAN DIASPORA BECKONS.

REFERENCES

Bennis, W. and Nanus B. (1985) *Leaders: The Strategies of Making Change* New York: Harper Row

Bloomfield, L. P. and Cleveland, H. "The Future of International Governance: Post-War Planning without having the War First," in *Journal of Development Planning*, No. 17, p.5

Bourne, Compton (1988) Commonwealth Secretariat/Caribbean Community Secretariat (London & Georgetown) *Caribbean Development to the Year 2000: Challenges, Prospects and Policies.*

Carrington, Edwin, (1989) *"Selected International Developments and Caribbean Interests in the Context of Its Membership in the ACP Group,"* Adlith Brown Memorial Lecture, Regional Programme of Monetary Studies, Jamaica: ISER, UWI.

Commonwealth Secretariat/Caribbean Community Secretariat, *Caribbean Development to the Year 2000: Challenges, Prospects and Policies.* (Main Author Compton Bourne), London, 1988.

Hook, S. (1943) *The Hero in History: A Study in Limitation and Possibility*, Boston: Beacon Press.

Keren, Michael (1988) Introduction to *IPSR* 9, 1, (January): 5.

Mazuri, Ali (1975) "The African University as a Multinational Corporation: Problems of Penetration and Dependency," *Harvard Educational Review*, 45 (May): 181–211

Migdal, Joel S., "Vision and Practice: The Leader, The State and the Transformation of Society", *International Political Science Review*, Vol. 9, January 1988, p. 24.

UNIDO, *Industry and Development: Global Report, 1988/89*, Vienna, 1988.

BRIEF BIOGRAPHY

NAME	John Edward Greene
DATE OF BIRTH	June 24 1939
ACADEMIC DEGREES	Ph.D. University of British Columbia (Political Science) 1969
	M.A. McMaster University (Political Science, 1964)
	B.Sc. University of London (Economics) 1962
ACADEMIC AFFILIATIONS	Director, Institute of Social and Economic Research
	Pro Vice Chancellor, University of the West Indies, Mona
BOOKS	*Race Versus Politics*, Institute of Social and Economic Research
	Small Business in Barbados: A Case of Survival (ISER, Eastern Caribbean, 1979)
	Peace, Security and Development (McMillan)
SELECTED ARTICLES	"Institutionalization of Party Systems" in Lewis (1976), pp 203–226
	"An Analysis of the General Election in Trinidad and Tobago, 1971" in Trevor Munroe and Rupert Lewis (eds) Readings in Government and Politics of the West Indies, University of the West Indies, January 1971

"The 1971 General Election in Barbados, *New World Quarterly*, 6, I, 1972

OTHER
INFORMATION

Memberships on Several Boards Including: —

Canadian Institute for International Peace and Security, Ottawa, Canada

Pan American Health Organization, Washington D.C. U.S.A.

National Commission for UNESCO, Kingston, Jamaica

Conclusion

CARIBBEAN VISIONS is a first collective effort of assessing the impact of the Caribbean Studies Association on the multi-disciplinary base of the Caribbean. The book records the visions of ten persons, each bringing aspects of his/her disciplinary emphasis to bear on the critical developmental trajectories along which the Caribbean region should travel. In all of the addresses, there is a concern for equity and democratic principles. The addresses span several years, several disciplines and several nationalities. Yet, in all of this manifold cultural, institutional and discipline-specific bias, a common thread runs. That thread is, we of the Caribbean region have to be always on guard, we have to constantly assess ourselves and we have to scope our long-term plans about where we came from as a people and where we would like to go.

On the surface, it would seem that there can be no unity in diversity. We believe that unity is evident in the works. For convenience we have three sections. We could have divided the presidents among nationalities. That would have been arbitrary and divisive. And such a division would have served no meaningful point.

The group has had a varied past. We see this in the fact that Bell, a U.S. National was born in Chicago but was raised in California and now spends his years in Massachusetts.

Lewis was born in Antigua but is a St. Lucian, indeed a Caribbean and international citizen. Palmer was born in Jamaica, but now spends his years in Washington D.C. Maingot, too, is a Caribbean national, having been born in Trinidad, but he now makes Florida home. Jones-Hendrickson was born in Sandy Point, St. Kitts, but after some years in Jamaica, he now calls St. Croix, Virgin Islands his home.

Andic born in Turkey, lived in Puerto Rico for many years. He now makes Washington, D.C. his home. Bourne was born in Guyana. For several years he lived in Jamaica, but Trinidad and Tobago is now his home. Young, the only living woman CSA President, was born in South Carolina. Her marital roots are Belizean. She now makes New Orleans her home. Serbin is from the greater Caribbean area. He was born in Argentina. He lives in Venezuela.

Finally, Greene, the last president in the group of ten, was born in Guyana but he now makes Jamaica his home.

The professional involvement of these ten presidents spans the globe in travel and is deep in commitment, massive in terms of community participation and prolific in terms of writing. Only a partial listing of the works of the presidents was given. On average, however, each President has written or edited two books, three or four monographs and over 20 articles in professionally referred journals. This type of involvement is testimony to the persons who have led the Caribbean Studies Association, the premier group that studies the Caribbean in all of its glory.

When all of the factors and facts behind the formation of the Caribbean Association are considered, its survival today, is a testament to many of the persons in this book and others who worked behind the scenes to keep the organization alive and well. Eddie Greene's conclusion is an appropriate note on which to end. "As a Caribbean family in the CSA (and the wider world), as scholars, as policy-makers, as

Caribbeanists, . . . together we can be the *architects of the ultimate visions.* A CARIBBEAN DIASPORA BECKONS." (Emphasis added).

CARIBBEAN VISIONS is a frontline testament of ten presidents of the Caribbean Studies Association. CARIBBEAN VISIONS, however, is also a holistic testament from the CSA family to the world family. CARIBBEAN VISIONS represents one step in the larger travel of life in the Caribbean and the Caribbean diaspora.

INDEX

Abbey, Marilyn 129
Adams, Grantley 107
Adams, Sam 8
Adams, Tom 108
Africa, 5,6,71,91,106,108,113,
African
  heritage 32
  names and apparel 93
  origins 13
Agee, Philip 18
Agricultural
  commodities 92
  employment 97
  enterprises 97
  exports 54
  productivity 79
  sector 55,79,97
Airborne Division, 101st 16
Albania 35
Alcoholic beverages 77
Alexander, Yonah 32
Alger, Janet Merrill 7,8
Allende, Salvador 18
Alliance for Progress economic
  programs 65
Alpers, Edward 121
America's backyard 52
American Declaration of
  Independence 17,23-4
American Mediterranean 52, 62
American security interests
  47-67
Andic, Fuat M 153, 160-1
Anguilla 125,127
Anti-Americanism 114
Antigua-and-Barbuda 37,90,
Argentina 59
Arkansas National Guard 16
Arms control 206,212

Asia 5,6,91,106
Asian Indians 104
Asian Indians. See also East
  Indians
Associated statehood 51
Association of Caribbean Studies
  153-4
Atlantic expansion 89
Authoritarian states 165
Authoritarianism 173-4,185-6
Ayub, Mahmood Ali 79

Bahamas 5,91,101
  house 101
Baldwin, James, 16
Bananas 54
Barbados 5,90,94,97,99,101,108,
  112
Barrall, Milton, Ambassador for
  U.S. Departments 50
Barrow, Errol 29,107,209
Barzun, Jacques 124
Basseterre demonstration (1950)
  130
Bauxite 48,49,53,54,57,64,
  industry 73
Belassa, Bela 77
Belize 37
Bell, Wendell 12,25,38,44-46
Best, Lloyd 28
Bhopal 225
Bird, Vere Sr. 125
Black Nationalist Party 16
Black Power Movement 93
  revolution, Haiti 111
Blanco, Jorge 108
Blythe, Hal 123
Bogle, Paul 17
Boldt, Menno 24

INDEX

Bollen, Kenneth A 36
Bourne, Compton 163,175-8
Bradshaw, Robert Llewellyn 122-46
   and the working class 135-6, 138-9
   bones in the rice, pepper in the soup 133-4
   British traits 139
   Caribbean integration 124-8
   communism 131-2
   nationalism 128-9
   principles, concerns, commitments 128,139-40
   speeches—excerpts 126,127, 131,137,141,142,143
   Statehood Day Address 1974 126
   Statehood Day Address 1976 142
   Statehood Day Address 1973 126
   strategies 143-4
Braithwaite, Lloyd 28
Brana-Shute, Gary 99
Brana-Shute, Rosemary 99
Brathwaite, Edward Kamau 121
Breuilly, John 129
Britain 10,107
British Guiana 112
   See also Guyana
British Labor Party 109
British Virgin Islands 91
Brown vs Board of Education of Topeka 15
Brown, H. Rap 16
Brzezinski 62
Bulgaria 38
Burnham, Forbes 49,108,111
Bustamante, Alexander 17,107
Butler, Uriah 119

Cacao 92
Canada 35,93
Canadian Indian movement 24

Caribbean Basin 89,109,184, 195-6
Caribbean Basin Initiative 85
Caribbean Commission 106
Caribbean Common Market States
   economic projections 229
Caribbean Common Market 97, 107,127,202-3
Caribbean Council of Churches 208-209
Caribbean development needs 187-9
Caribbean Development Bank(CDB) 104,187
Caribbean development 223-4, 232-41
Caribbean foreign policy 51,57-8
Caribbean identity 195-8
Caribbean integration 124-8,145
Caribbean labor movement 132
   See also Trade union movement
Caribbean Sea 52,89
Caribbean Studies Association 181,221-3,230,232-41,245-8
Caribbean Zone of Peace 206-217
   obstacles 212-7
Caribbean, Post Independence 123-7,141
Caribbean-Central American relations 62,63,64
CARICOM 49,60,104,127
Carter, Jimmy President 18
   Carter administration 58,59
Carter-Young-Vance 58
Cayenne 113
Cayman Islands 91
Central America 51,52,59,62,63, 66,67
   ports 101
   railroads 101
Central High School, Little Rock, Arkansas 15,16

INDEX 251

Cesaire, Aime 28,37,109,111
Chaguaramas Treaty 127
Chambers, George 108
Charles, Mary Eugenia 108
Chernobyl 225
Chocolate manufacturing industry, Hershey, Pennsylvania 78
Christian Democrats 104
Christianity 98
Christophe, Henri 139
Church 98
CIA 18
Cipriani, Andrew 109
Citrus 54
Civil rights 15,21,114
Civil Rights Act of 1964 16
Civil service 100
Clark Amendment 58
Cleaver, Eldridge 16
Cocoa beans 78
Coffee 54
Colombia 89,112
Colonialism 3,12,55,71,106,111, 155-6
Commercial banks 80
 loans 80
Committee of 21 94
Commonwealth of Caribbean Conference (1976) 125
Communist bloc 57
Communists of Great Britain 131
Condorcet 28
Consent of the governed 8,23,24
Constitutionalism 8
CORE 16
Council for Mutual Economic Assistance (COMECON) 57
Creole dialect, Haiti 102
Crile, George 17
Cuba 7,47,48,49,51,52,53,57,61, 62,90,98,103,104,108,112,114
 relations with the Caribbean 57,59-62

U.S. problems 59
Cuban "expansionism" 51
Cuban Revolution 112,113
Curacao 29,99,101

Debt, Caribbean 228
Decolonization 106-7,112,113
Democracy 7,182-190,206
Democratic-pluralist states 165
Democratic-pluralist systems 165-74
Democratic
 revolution 6-8
 socialism 56,108
Deosaran, Ramesh 121
Dependency syndrome 187
Dessalinean Black Revolution 110
Destabilization 58
Detente 59
Development resources 158-60
Direct-dial telephones 101
Divorce bill 109
Domestic market 54,76,77
Dominica 5,62,65,90,94,108
 attempted invasion, 1981 102
Dominican Republic 7,47,66,90, 94,108,112
Downing, Carlos A 128
Duvalier, Francois (Papa Doc) 111,139
Duvalier, Jean Claude (Baby Doc) 111

East Germany 38
East Indians 20,103,104
 in Trinidad 93
Eastern Caribbean Common Market 97,107
Economic growth 50,54,55,56, 79,158
Economic patron 166-8
Economic regulation 169-72
Education, 12,13,101,189-90
 goals 189-90

252 INDEX

primary 12
university 101
Egalitarian revolution 11-19
Eisenhower, President 15,16
El Salvador 38,89
Emigration 83,97,98,101
Employment 50,76,97
  Caribbean 76,84
  Jamaica 80,82
  Employment. See also
    Unemployment
Energy crisis 97
Equality 11,14-37
Equity 19-28
Ethnic divisions 103
Europe 6,63,76,89
  Eastern reforms 226
European Economic Community 48
European Enlightenment 8
Evers, Medger 16
Exports 71,73,84,85
  markets 50,76,77,84,85
Extra-legal families 12
Family 102

Farrell, Trevor 75
Faubus, Orval, Governor, Arkansas 15,16
Fontaine, Pierre-Michelle 121
Ford regime 58
Foreign markets. See
  Exports—Markets
Free World Congress—Official Report (1949) 131
Freedom riders 16
French Canada 5
French Communist Party 109
French Guiana 113
French West Indies 101,113

Gairy, Eric 94
Garvey, Marcus 17
Gas 107
GDP 91

Dominican Republic 156
Honduras 155
U.S. 226
Global crises 225
GNP 30
Ethiopia 155
Jamaica 155
Gomes, Albert 144
Gordon, William George 17
Greene, J. E. 100,221,241-243
Grenada 5,51,61,62,90,94,113, 185
  invasion 38,96
  Revolution (1979) 96
Grenadines 5
Gross Domestic Product (GDP) 91
  Dominican Republic 156
  Honduras 155
  U.S. 226
  Ethiopia 155
Gross National Product (GNP) 30
  Jamaica 155
Group of Eight 211
Group of Seven Countries 226
Guadeloupe 5,90
Guatemala 38
Guyana 5,20,32,47,49,57,58,61, 62,97,103,108
Guzman, Antonio 66,108

Haiti 6,89,90,97,98,100,101,108, 111,112
  literacy 100
Hayes, Carlton J. H. 6
Hector, Tim 121
Hickenlooper amendment 49
Hinduism 103,111
Honduras 35,38
Hooker, Richard 166
Hotel industry 73
Human capital 78,84,85
Human resources 153-5
Human rights. See Civil rights

INDEX 253

Hume, David 131
Hungary 38
Hydro-electricity schemes 64

Ideological pluralism 57
Illegal drugs 53
Illegal emigration 53
Illegitimate children 12-13
  illegitimacy rate 99
Illiteracy 55
  Haiti 100
IMF 226
Immigration, legal and illegal 53
Indentured labor 6
Independent sovereign states 4-5,112
Indians (American Indians) 104
Indigenous engine of growth 71-85
Indigenous industrial development 77
Industrial incentives 79,81
Industrial strike, Curacao (1969) 99-100
Industrialization by invitation strategies 72
Inequality 3,11,12,13,19-28
Inequity 22-8
Inflation rate
  Jamaica 80
Interest rate 80
International Centre for Settlement of Investment Disputes (ICSID) 49
International economic order 14, 36
International labor organizations 104
International Monetary Fund(IMF) 60,61
International trade markets projections 227
Investment 53,54,55,57,79,157
  Jamaica 82,54
Iran-Contra scandal 38

Islam 105

Jagan, Cheddi 49,107,111
Jamaica 5,12,15,33,34,47,48,49, 50,51,5355,56,56,57,58,60,61, 62,64,65,71,73,74,77,79,80,82, 90,93,94,97,100,101,108,112
Jamaica Labour Party 34
James, C. L. R. 28,110,121,133, 138
Jamesian view 138
Japan 78
Jasso, Guillermina 25
Jim Crow laws 114
Jimenez, Perez 112
Joint-venture arrangements 72
Jones-Hendrickson, S. B. 121, 149-51

Kane, Edward 172
Kenyatta, Jomo 106,113
Kissinger, Henry 52
  regime 58
Kohn, Hans 6

L'Ouverture, Toussaint 110,121, 139
Labor 55,54-76,97
Labor force 98
  Jamaica 81,83
Labor surplus, Caribbean 71-85
Labor unions 83,100
  See also trade unions
Land ownership 98-99
Lane, Robert E 34
Latin America 6,47,63,64,91,106, 107,200,210
  and the Caribbean 202-4
Leeward Islands 90,91
Legal families 12
Legitimacy of government 29-34
Legitimate children 12
Lenin 95
Lewis, Vaughan A 67-9,145-6
Lewis, W. Arthur 79,121

INDEX

Light manufacturing industries 79
Linz, Juan J 29
Lipset, Seymour Martin 7,29
Literacy 12,83,91,100
Local ownership 72-3,76
Lome Convention 49

Machinery and equipment industry 78
Maingot, Anthony P 100,115-7
Malcolm X 16
Manchester, William 16
Manley administration 54
Manley, Michael 28,56,108,122, 124,139-40
Manley, Norman W 17,107,111, 158
Mannheim, Karl 95
Manufacturing 77-85
 industries 77-85
 small establishments 81
Market failure 170
Marti, Jose 103
Martinique 5,90,101,109
Marx, Karl 27-28
Marxism 50,51,103,109,110,111
Martriarchical society 99
McCartheyism 15
McNamara, Robert 65
Meredith, James 16
Mestizos 104
Mexico 63,64,67,89,104
Middle income countries 50
Migration 83,97,98,101
Military aid 212
 United States 184-6
Military repression 185-6
Mineral
 industries 64
 resources 53
Mintz, Sidney 194
Modern conservative societies 89-114
Montserrat 91

MPLA 60
Multinational corporations 29, 33,35
Munoz Marin, Luis 158
Muslim 103
Myrdal, Gunnar 167,172,173

Naipaul, V. S. 12
Nanny of the Maroons 17
Nassau Understanding, July 1984 159
Nation-state 34-5
National representation abroad 102
National sovereignty 10,17
Nationalist movements 8-10
 conditions for formation 9-10
Nationalism 72-3
Natural resources
 El Salvador 156
 Hong Kong 156
Negritude 109
Negroes 104
Nehru 106
Neruda, Pablo 187
Netherlands Antilles 5,90,99, 101,112
Nevis 99
New Jewel Movement 61
New states 3,4-6,11,36,38,47,48
Newton, Huey P 16
Nicaragua 51,62,185
Nixon regime 58
Nixon-Kissinger-Ford regime 58
Nkrumah, Kwame 106,113
Non-Aligned Group of Nations 14
Non-alignment 56
Norriega, Manuel Antonio 38
North America 7,76,84
North Atlantic 53
North-South 36
Nunes, Frederick 173-174
Nyerere, Julius 113

OAS 49
OECS 104,202
Oil 107
 production, Trinidad 50,92
 revenues, Trinidad 93
OPEC 92,107
Operation Blackburne 130
OPIC 49
Organization of American States 49
Organization of Eastern Caribbean States (OECS) 104,202
Overseas Private Investment Corporation (OPIC) 49

Pacific 5,6
Palmer, Ransford W 86-7
Panama 5,38
 Canal 52,59,101
Papa Bradshaw. See Bradshaw, Robert LLewellyn
Papiamento (Curacao) 102
Parks, Rosa 16
Peace in the Caribbean 193
Peace, Caribbean 193,205,206-7
 See also Caribbean Zone of Peace
People's National Movement, Trinidad 94
People's National Party, Jamaica 33,56
Perestroika 227
Petroleum 52,60,62,78
Pinilla, Rojas 112
Plural society 28
Poland 38
Political democracy 6-8,11
Political elite 55
Political independence 8-9,71,72
Political orientation 54-59
Political patronage 167-8
Political regimes
 authoritarian states 165
 classifications 164-5

INDEX 255

 democratic-pluralist states 165
 populist-statist states 165
Political stability 56
Popular Movement for the Liberation of Angola (MPLA) 60
Population
 density, Dominican Republic 155
 density, Ethiopia 155
 density, Honduras 155
 density, Jamaica 155
 Jamaica 81
 racial structure 104
Populism 56
Populist-statist states 165
Porter, John 24
Portugal 35
Posner, Richard 170
Post-independence Caribbean 123-7,141
Poverty 75
 persistent 28
Public service 100
Public transportation
 London 101
Puerto Rico 5,79,90,98,103,113,114

Race 6,111
 conflict 103
Racial segregation 75
 structure 104
Rastafarian Movement 105
Rational choosers 24
Raw materials 76,78
Rawls, John 24,136
Rawlsian principle 134,136,142
Reagan administration 184
Reagan diplomacy 62-66
Redemocratization 183-4
Religiosity 98
Rhodesia 10
Rigged elections 32
Robinson, Robert V 12,25,34

INDEX

Rodney, Walter 28,93
 Rodney riots 50,55
Rohlehr, Gordon 121
Romania 38
Rossi, Peter H 25
Rubin, Vera 193
Russett, Bruce 38

Salamon, Lester 171
Salimu 138
Santeria 98
Santo Domingo 103
Scandinavia 36
Schlesinger, Arthur 58
Seaga, Edward 108
Serbin, Andres 193,218-20
Shango 98
Sharpe, Sam 17
Siegfried, John 171
Slave trade 106
Smith, Adam 28
SNCC 16
Snell, Jim 123
Social change 186-7
Social crisis 54-9
Social justice 3-37
Socialism 56,109
Socialist bloc 57
Socialist International 104
South America 200-1,206,211, 212
Southern Christian Leadership Conference 16
Soviet Union 35,38,59
Spain 36,89
St Kitts-Nevis 37,94
St Kitts-Nevis-Anguilla 90,123, 130,143
 economy 136,141
 sugar industry 136-7
St Lucia 5,61,90,94
St Vincent 5,90,94,99
State-people relationship 163-174
 economic aspects 163

Stevenson, David L 12
Stone, Carl 164,167,173
Strikes, St. Kitts 135
 agricultural 135
 seven-week 135
 thirteen-week 135
Sugar 54,92
 industry 73,136-7
Surinam 5,101,103,113
 Revolution (1980) 96
Sweet, Charlie 123

Taiwan 36
Taki-taki (Surinam) 102
Tapia Group in Trinidad 28
Television 101
Third World 14,18,28,38,63,67, 110
Thomas, Clive Yolande 76
Tobacco 54,77
 products 77
Toffler, Alvin 35
Tourism 48,49,54
Trade 52,53,76,89
 potentials 227-8
 trade restraints 226,228
Trade union movement 55,132
Trade unions 55,131
Trade unions. See also Labor unions
Treaty of Chaguaramas 127
Trinidad and Tobago 5,15,20,28, 47,50,56,90,92,94,97,98,100, 101,103,105,107,108,109,112
Trinidad labor movement uprising 1937 110
Trinidad Rebellion (1970) 50,56, 93
Turks and Caicos Islands 91
Two party system 56

Underdevelopment, characteristics of 74
Underemployment 12,75
Unemployable 55,75

INDEX 257

Unemployed 56,99
Jamaica 74-5
Unemployment 12,55,64,97
 rate 74
 rate, Jamaica 74,79
 Trinidad and Tobago 75,92,93
Unemployment. See also Employment
UNIDO 226
United Labor Force, Trinidad (ULF) 94
United States 15,16,17,18,47-67, 93,101,104,113,114,184
 diplomatic relations 51
 economic interests in the Caribbean 59-67
 interests 52-4
 relations with Caribbean 47-67
 security interests in the Caribbean 47-67
United States Virgin Islands 90
Universal adult suffrage 8,55
University of the West Indies 101

Venezuela-Cuba-USSR trade arrangement 60
Vietnam war 58
Violence in strike action, use of 110
Visionary leadership models 230-1

Voodoo 98

Wages 55
 rates 82
 rates, Jamaica 82
Walster, Elaine 25
Ward, Barbara 224
Watergate 58
Weber, Max 100
West African religions 98
West Indies Federation 71,103, 107,112
Westminister parliamentary system 57,173
Whites 104
Williams, Eric 28,93,105-8,110, 111,158,187
Windward and Leeward Islands self-government 130
Windward Islands 90
Women
 unemployed, Jamaica 75
World Bank 49,97
World War II 4,15

Young, Alma 181,190-2
Young-Vance 62
Youth 55
 employment 92
 labor force 98
 unemployed 99
Yugoslavia 35,36

Zimbabwe 10

ORDER FORM

POLITICS AND ECONOMICS:

(1) CARIBBEAN VISIONS: Ten Presidential Addresses of Ten Presidents of the Caribbean Studies Association. Contributions by Wendell Bell, Vaughan Lewis, Ransford Palmer, Anthony Maingot, S. B. Jones-Hendrickson, Compton Bourne, Alma H. Young, Andres Serbin and J. Edward Greene. ISBN 0-932831-06-0. (ECI, 1991). Publication price: $25.95. AVAILABLE JUNE 1991.

(2) A PROFILE OF FREDERIKSTED, ST. CROIX, U.S. VIRGIN ISLANDS (with suggestions for revitalization). A detailed political and economic assessment of the second town of Frederiksted, St. Croix. Published by the Caribbean Research Institute, University of the Virgin Islands. (CRI, 1990). Price: US$10.95.

(3) INTERVIEWS WITH LEE L. MOORE. (Interviewer Dawud Byron). Fourteen frank interviews with Lee L. Moore, former Premier of St. Kitts-Nevis Labour Party in a holistic developmental policy for St. Kitts-Nevis. ISBN 0-932831-01-X. (ECI, 1989). Price: US$10.95.

(4) PUBLIC FINANCE AND MONETARY POLICY IN OPEN ECONOMIES. (By S. B. Jones-Hendrickson). A systematic treatment of the integration of fiscal and monetary policy in open economies. Special emphasis is placed on the Commonwealth Caribbean. The work addresses the inequalities which exist between and among classes in the Third World. Published by the Institute of Social and Economic Research, (ISER), Jamaica. (ISER, 1985). Price: US$15.95.

(5) READINGS IN CARIBBEAN PUBLIC SECTOR ECONOMICS. (Edited by Fuat Andic and S. B. Jones-Hendrickson). A series of essays by internationally renowned experts and scholars in the field of public finance and taxation. The essays relate to the Caribbean and the Third World. (ISER, 1981). Price: US$10.95.

Telephone Orders: (809) 772-1011
Fax Orders: (809) 772-3665
Postal Orders: Eastern Caribbean Institute, P.O. Box 1338
Frederiksted St. Croix, USVI 00841

Please send the following books. I understand that I may return any books for a full refund—for any reason, no questions asked.

_____

_____

_____

☐ Please send me a free catalog

Shipping:

Book Rate: $1.75 for the first book and 75 cents for each additional book. (Surface Shipping may take three to four weeks)

Air Mail: $3.00 per book

Payment:
☐ Check   ☐ Money Order